Bells Across Cardigan Bay

THE MEMOIR OF A
BORTH MASTER MARINER

Dedicated to:

Terry Davies
Borth's most knowledgeable historian of its mariner life

William Troughton
for being the faithful guardian of the
National Library of Wales' maritime information

Chris Holden
for his useful research of life under water

Peter Fowler
for unending patience on the long journey
to the mysteries of the past

Bells Across Cardigan Bay

THE MEMOIR OF A
BORTH MASTER MARINER

J A N   W I L L I A M S

First impression: 2022

'Cardigan Bay' used with the permission The Society of Authors as
the Literary Representatives of the Estate of John Masefield

Cover design: Y Lolfa

ISBN: 978 1 80099 259 7

Published and printed in Wales
on paper from well-maintained forests by
Y Lolfa Cyf., Talybont, Ceredigion SY24 5HE
website www.ylolfa.com
e-mail ylolfa@ylolfa.com
tel 01970 832 304
fax 832 782

Contents

Part IV: The Final Disgrace   135

Praise Song to Cardigan Bay and its Master Mariners   152

Appendix   154

Cardigan Bay

Clean, green, windy billows, notching out the sky,
Grey clouds tattered into rags, sea-winds blowing high,
And the ships under topsails, beating, thrashing by,
And the mewing of the herring gulls.

Dancing, flashing green seas shaking white locks,
Boiling in blind eddies over hidden rocks,
And the wind in the rigging, the creaking of the blocks,
And the straining of the timber hulls.

Delicate, cool sea-weeds, green and amber-brown,
In beds where shaken sunlight slowly filters down
On many a drowned seventy-four, many a sunken town,
And the whitening of the dead men's skulls.

This poem by the Englishman John Masefield is an evocative introduction to the world of the master mariner. Here is a fitting introduction to this voyage of discovery.

Part I

The Author's Story

PREFACE

The bells chime out

AND SO IT begins, the bells chime out, and the voyage commences.

It's a voyage into the world of the master mariners of Cardigan Bay, above all the 'worthy captain', John Evans of Saxatile, Borth, my own great-grandfather. At the core of his life was the dramatic sinking of his brig, the *Rowland Evans*. What really happened to that splendid ship and what is so intriguing about the life of that particular master mariner?

My fascination with his story began when I was eleven years old. A captain's medical chest was brought down from an attic, and three old ladies, my grandmother and two great-aunts, told me the tale of how it was rescued from the wreck of their father's ship, the *Rowland Evans*, in 1882. A wreck! Now that sounded dramatic, and the gruesome medical instruments had their own fascination to a child.

It was when I started to look more carefully at the forbidding portrait that hung in the house of John and Sarah Evans that I wondered what sort of people they could have been. All around were fine collections of nautical objects, and splendid portraits of two fine sailing ships. I wanted to know more. Everything seemed to have a link to the sea. It seemed the constant companion in their lives, both friend and enemy.

The real shock of the captain's secret life, however, did not reveal itself to me until 2010 when, by accident, I discovered the work of Terry Davies about Borth's maritime history. He mentioned that Captain John Evans had been disciplined by a naval inquiry. Worst of all, he had lost his master's certificate for a year! Whatever had he done wrong? This sounded rather shaming. Why had the mystery been hidden? Nobody in the family had said anything about this!

Captain John Evans, the third of three generations of master mariners, all with the same name of John Evans, came from the village of Borth in Ceredigion. A remarkable number of master mariners have lived there over the years.

My great-grandfather initially lived in a smallholding in Cwmcethin, on the outskirts of a village known as Glan-y-wern. Later he moved to the attractive Georgian house now known as Saxatile, Borth, when he married in 1854. This was the house I had learnt to love as a child, and it was the home of the three sisters whom I knew as my grandmother and two great-aunts. It was the stories that they told me which inspired me to want to know more about my ancestors. They obviously had a deep respect for their father and loved to tell the tale of how he and their mother escaped that wreck in 1882 off the Welsh coast with the crew, and actually rowed all the way home to Borth. Surely, a great adventure!

Slowly I unearthed an amazing amount of information about the worthy captain from many different sources. At the National Library of Wales in Aberystwyth there were detailed references to his life as a captain, his crew lists and log books. I found out how he dealt with drunken sailors and inexperienced seaman, the muddles he got into with his log books, which were duly investigated by the authorities. That correspondence, in particular, was hilarious, and well worth reading.

Eventually, I tracked down accounts of his disciplinary hearing in the newspapers of the time, and here, at last, it seemed that the worthy captain's secret was to be revealed.

In the process I gained a real insight into my family's

history and how my own life has been shaped. It has given me a vivid picture of the life of the master mariners of Cardigan Bay, especially Borth, in the latter nineteenth century. Above all, the village was linked to a never-ending flow of legendary stories, which is a remarkable heritage.

INTRODUCTION

The sands of time –
my memories of Borth

IN THE AUTUMN of 2010 I took my partner Peter on a visit to the glorious Borth beach of my childhood. I had not been back there since 1999. We went for a specific reason. I was on a search for my great-grandfather, but somehow our walk through the village provoked a strange mixture of memories from my own life. It was also a way of introducing my dear friend to my family background in this unique village of master mariners.

When I was a small child frolicking on the beach, summers seemed to pass in splendid sunshine. Yet there were hard winters too, when it became a place of fierce winds and sharp rainfall. Even in August we were rarely without gusts of wind. As time had passed I found that the village seemed to have lost most of its magic for me. Many houses had become second homes, or were otherwise very rundown. When I left home in Borth to start a career as a teacher, my mother was on her own in a house that was damp and in need of repair. There was a terrible sense of loneliness, as many of the old families with their wonderful seafaring tales were dying out. Therefore, investigating the past of the master mariners was going to be a challenge for me.

Peter and I travelled to Borth the way I had always travelled in my childhood – by train. From Euston there was nothing very beautiful about the English stretch of that journey but, beyond Shrewsbury, the loveliness of Wales opened up. There was enchantment while passing through the lush green fields of Montgomeryshire. Then, suddenly, it felt as if the sky lightened up as we neared the wonders of the Dyfi estuary. Here there were evocative cries of sea birds, the strange-shaped pools of the marshes where sheep grazed and, at last, the throb of delight as the railway line became long and straight and took us into the straggle of houses at the side of the sea that was Borth. I was delighted on that day. The sun was shining and I could show Peter the village at its best.

We did not stop to look more closely from the station platform, although there are captivating views facing inland to the golden reeds of Cors Fochno and its wild ponies and the dainty picturesque St Matthew's church. We were only vaguely aware that there were more people than I seemed to remember getting off the train with bundles of their shopping. There was a sense of a younger community having come to live there.

We bustled past them. We had one thing in mind. We wanted so much to see the beach! So, out of the station entrance we raced down Cambrian Terrace with its rows of ageing Victorian villas and on towards the sea.

The beach

The beach lay ahead of us and, as the tide was out, it was at its fullest extent and stretched for miles in front of us. The sky was blue and the sea itself was turquoise, with the added depths of green-grey. Frothy, white waves lapped lazily on the beach. Slithering and sliding down the stones, we found our feet sinking into the soft sand which was empty and welcoming, but we had to be careful to avoid tripping over old weathered groynes.

In front of us were the splendid cliffs with the war memorial looking peculiarly, from a distance, like a beer bottle. That southern headland is known as Craig yr Wylfa or the 'Cliff of Waiting', where Borth's womenfolk were known to wait for their men as they returned from catching herring in Victorian times.

I slipped out of my shoes and socks and ran to the sea for a paddle in the freezing water.

'Trying to be King Maelgwn?' Peter laughed.

I had forgotten that he had seen family photographs of Borth carnival, with revelers sitting on chairs trying to defeat the sea, just as they had done in the ancient days when King Maelgwn and his fellow courtiers had clung on to their chairs in the waves to prove how long they could stay out there in order to make themselves king of Gwynedd.

Just as Peter and I turned to look if we could see the submerged forest, I heard a ghost's voice nearer to my time saying, 'You never loved the beach as much as I did.' I recognised it as an echo of something my mother used to say when she had a wave of 'hiraeth', or longing, for Borth after she moved to my home in Brightlingsea. She was wrong. We just had different memories of the beach.

I actually loved the sea because I could swim. My mother was never able to swim because her redhead's delicate skin would break out into a rash in saltwater. I was lucky that, when I was eleven years old, I was taught to swim by the father of Gill Thacker, one of my summer holiday friends. Bless you Mr Thacker, for instilling in me the courage to go in the water and make progress with my feeble breaststroke. It was a vast improvement from simply sitting in the shallows in my baggy woolly swimming costume, nibbling at tomato sandwiches.

I grew to love those high tides in August when I could throw myself onto the back of the gigantic waves and be almost swept into the shore with no effort on my part. It was almost like surfing, but without a board. There were strange companions in the water, like jellyfish and mackerel that you could catch with your hands because they came in so close to land.

Summer evenings could be especially lovely when the porpoises gamboled and jumped out of the water. The setting sun made a golden pathway through the waves – enough to inspire tales of mermaids and mariners! Even on a grey winter's day, taking a solitary walk by the edge of a tempestuous sea could fill the imagination with maritime adventures.

I loved the cliffs and the rock pools. Surprisingly, for a timid child, I would scramble along the ledges of the cliff face looking for caves. I was always hoping for a glimpse of 'y ladi wen', the white lady, the mysterious creature who lurked in the caves. The rock pools were full of colourful creatures. I have to confess to a terrible crime; I had a passion for sticking my finger into sea anemones' mouths to tease them into thinking they had something tasty to eat. I never caught enough shrimps to make a decent tea. It was our paying summer guests from London who could catch and cook enough shrimps for eight people!

I loved the people I met on the beach. There was Emlyn the Donkeys, who was too busy reciting poetry in the pub to bother with taking money from the punters. He had a passion for reciting Edgar Allan Poe's poem 'The Raven'. He would fling his big leather pouch to my friends and I, and we would take charge of the donkeys on the beach for him. I loved Betty, the small black donkey, best.

On one occasion we rescued Emlyn from experiencing a fatal accident. We were coming round the corner in Glan-y-wern when my father caught a glimpse of Emlyn's black and white sheepdog. He braked quickly enough to stop hitting him.

When my father died when I was 14, Emlyn came to our house and pressed a crumpled and dirty five pound note into my mother's hand, saying, 'for the little girl'.

There were two boys from Birmingham who stayed in the house next to ours. They made a wonderful discovery: a penguin that came out of the sea. We did not know what to do with it, so we put it back in the waves. I wonder how it got there and whether it found its way home.

Young students came down in August and ran an Evangelical Christian mission. It ran an amazing number of events, especially popular with youngsters. The most popular was something called 'sausage sizzles', which were stories around the campfire. They used to sing the most stirring choruses.

'Will your anchor hold in the storms of life,
when the clouds unfold their wings of strife?'

I was very vulnerable to the charms of the young student preachers. I think I got 'converted' at least three times! Somehow, I felt joyous by coming to Jesus. I may have found religion a little comforting in my early teens after my father, uncle, grandmother, and two great-aunts died in close proximity. Somehow, I had to survive that succession of funeral teas and the loss of family.

No doubt my great-grandfather, Captain John Evans, would have known such songs. They might have cheered him up in some exotic foreign port, although he never had enough Welshmen on the *Rowland Evans* to have a really rousing chorus.

Singing continued with evening hymn singing at the Public Hall in Borth on Sundays. Amusingly, as teenagers many of us went to the Band of Hope, an old Temperance organisation with strong religious roots, which seemed to have little effect on us as we walked home trying to sing pop songs to prove that we were in fact trendy! I saw little evidence among that group of teetotalism in adult life. In fact, quite the opposite! If anything, there were a large number of heavy drinkers.

The walk up to the cliff

One of the glories of the village was the walk to the cliff, where you saw such a glorious spread of breathtakingly lovely landscapes. In the far distance were the blue and purple hills that lay behind Aberdyfi. Sometimes you caught glimpses of the entire Llŷn peninsula, even seeing Bardsey Island, which was to play so important a part in the captain's saga. That stretch, of what seemed like a kind of a finger stretching out into the ocean, suggested some supernatural power.

Talking of Aberdyfi, I did remember the awkward curve of the railway line when you had to change at Dovey Junction in order to join another line to make a visit to Aberdyfi. There was something very exciting about emerging from the tunnel at Penhelig and seeing that spruce little town of Aberdyfi, with its freshly-painted houses. Here was prosperity, and feasts of potted shrimp and sea trout. Splendid sailing boats of leisure sailors bobbed on the sea.

Then there were also the glories of Ynyslas overlooking the Dyfi estuary. My grandmother used to go searching for cockles there. She explained how she would scrape the sand over the blowholes to reveal the cockles just below the surface. Then, when she got them home, she would place them in a bucket of clean water with a handful of porridge oats or bran, and leave them overnight; then boil them so that they would be fit to eat. Ynyslas sand dunes are now part of the Dyfi National Nature Reserve and UNESCO Dyfi Biosphere Reserve. As a child I only knew it as a glorious playground, a place for gamboling among the sand dunes and for having grand picnics.

We adored that marvellous high dune which you could slide down, but very cautiously avoided the spikes of Marram grass sticking into your bottom. The landscape of the dunes continually changed, so a game of hide-and-seek was always a challenge. We were lucky we never got lost for long.

As you walk from Ynyslas to Borth you pass the links golf course which dates back to 1885. As a young woman my mother boasted a fine set of golf clubs, and admired the dashing young men in their plus fours and smart jerseys who propped up the bar there. My generation always regarded the golfers with distain. We dismissed them as

English and snobs, and far too sophisticated for us because they had white telephones when everybody else had black telephones.

From the cliff we could see how Borth itself stretched out, its one main street along the wondrous curve of the shingle bay. Behind it lay the peat marshes of Cors Fochno which translates from Welsh as the Fenland of Pigs. Most people now call it Borth bog.

Today it inspires naturalists and folklore enthusiasts, but it needs an expert to explore it properly, for it has been known for people to disappear into the slurp of the treacherous peat. It is in fact a raised bog at sea level, which means it has been built up more rapidly by rainwater.

The bog is home to plenty of unusual flora and fauna, including birds, butterflies, moths and plants. The sensations that I remembered best were the beautiful sounds of sky larks disappearing high up into the blue yonder, and the menace of adders courting in the spring. I loved the soft white flax of the reeds and wondered how they were used to make the old reed candlesticks in our kitchen. Now, apparently, you can find otters, red kites, small red damselfly, rosy marsh moth, bush cricket and three species of the sundews plant there. As a child, what I found most fascinating was the sundews stretching out to trap insects.

Yet, the really fearsome creatures to me had appeared in the folklore of Cors Fochno. It included a character called the old hag (gwrach in Welsh) of Borth bog.

The gwrach was said to be seven foot high, thin, bony and yellow-cheeked, moving like a serpent. She had teeth as black as the long wavy hair on her large head, hair which fell in waves down her back. It was her fault, apparently, that 'shaking sickness' effected people in the area. This sickness was a fever which especially inflicted the young and the old. It began with a patient feeling sickly, then their body beginning to shake and they were speechless. It lasted for an hour a day, but then increased up to eight to ten hours a day as the days went by, until the shaking stopped and people began to regain their strength.

Apparently, the hag only made her appearance in the dead of night, because she was so embarrassed by her appearance. Teachers told their pupils to keep their windows closed at night to prevent the hag slipping in and spreading the fever. Another preventive measure was to stop burning peat, because that disturbed 'yr hen wrach'.

The disease apparently began to fade in 1900. This may have been because the bog was being reclaimed and drained, and the villagers were burning coal instead of cutting peat. The scientists said that the insects that carried malaria were dying out with the decrease in the size of the bog. So it seems that mixed up with a folk tale came a genuine description of an illness. But, of course, there is nothing like the story of 'yr hen wrach' for providing entertainment.

She is just as fascinating as that other set-piece for storytellers, 'the old toad of Borth bog'. This tells of how an eagle wanted to marry an owl because she was old and a more trustworthy bride than a flighty young chick. In the story the eagle questions a long list of creatures, including a toad, about the age of the owl. They tell the eagle about their memories. The old folk always said you could ask a toad to foretell your future, just as the eagle did.

On that day in 2010, we only went as far as the war memorial to enjoy the magnificent views of the bay. I had always been a little nervous when passing that great cleft in the cliff beyond the monument, which always gave me vertigo. Yet, somehow, I would find the courage to go down to the seclusion and peace of Aberwenol Bay, where there would be the occasional visit of a seal.

The next bay beyond it was called Wallog, where the Sarn Gynfelyn split of land stuck out to sea. This is, in fact, a natural feature, but the Sarn may have been built to reclaim land from the sea. It is a special place, for there is a folk tale, which I shall tell you later, that notes that this causeway leads to the magical land of Rhys Ddwfn.

Sadly, it was a story that I did not hear as a child. So I was delighted when I found the enthralling storyteller Peter Stevenson (who has made a video for Vimeo, the video-hosting internet company) using the Borth landscape as the background to the story, and also fiddle music to create a dream-like atmosphere. Maybe our family, like a lot of Welsh families, was nervous of the fairies whom they called 'y tylwyth teg', which means fair people. They were certainly to be addressed as such in order to show proper respect, as they were known to play mischievous tricks on mortal folk.

The village High Street – our old homes

Peter and I hurried down from the cliff path in order to explore the village itself and find the houses where I had lived:

London House: I was born in 1943 on a cold May day; they had to light a fire in the tiny maternity hospital in Aberystwyth. Not long after I was taken back to the home of my grandparents, Sarah Mary and W.T. Lewis, in Borth, to a house called London House.

Everyone was shocked that I was only four pounds in weight at birth, but I went on to become a bouncing baby! London House, in the days of its glory, was a magnificent general store. My mother used to say it sold anything from tin tacks to fur coats. On the day of our visit in 2010, a quick look at the signs on the sides of the house bore the scars of its many reincarnations. On one side it said 'the Welsh Kitchen', but above the door it declared it was a Tandoori restaurant! What would my grandfather have said? As a Welsh speaker, he had struggled to learn English in midlife in order to serve the summer visitors. This was as far as he wanted to mix with 'foreigners'.

Ardwyn: Strangely, as we passed Ardwyn, I noticed that it was now looking spruce and far more attractive than I had remembered it. In fact, most of the houses on the sea side of the road looked well cared for and freshly painted. We could see from the beach side that many houses now boasted large glass windows and balconies so that they could enjoy views of the sea. It looked, at last, as though there were more permanent residents and fewer second homes.

We moved into Ardwyn when I was four years old. We had moved from Warwickshire after my father became ill with a chest complaint. My father had a job he loved, a lecturer at a girls' horticultural college in Studley, a rather splendid institution for well-bred country girls who needed an education to manage agricultural and horticultural estates.

It was a sad arrival in Borth, for by now my grandfather was in his final days. I have a clear memory of his lying dying, so his death rattle shook his brass bed.

To me Ardwyn seemed a rather depressing house. There was so much Victoriana – large cases of stuffed birds, heavy fire irons and a gigantic mirror above the fireplace with a frame curving into gilt fish heads. I found them all so ugly. Even when we gave the stuffed birds to the primary school, I found them there, years later, unloved, upside down and shoved in a corner. I must admit I felt that was the fate they deserved.

There was, however, one compensating feature of Ardwyn – the glory of watching the magnificent setting suns from the back of the house.

It might explain why I was such a nervous and serious-minded child. Gradually, however, I grew to love being able to run down to the beach just out of the back door, and there were odd moments when we had grand company. The local MP addressed the villagers from the steps of our house to thank them for voting for him. Politicians at election times then were keener to meet people face to face.

Saxatile: Sadly, when we reached the lovely Georgian house that had been Captain John Evans' home, we found it was now battling with damp. And what had happened to those lovely brass letters on the wall that had spelt out its name? I did not want to remember the house like this! We'd inherited it from the great-aunts after their death and had sold Ardwyn. Strangely, just after this, I had started at Ardwyn Grammar School.

Saxatile was a house I loved, with its handsome late Georgian proportions (which had given it the right to be a Grade II listed building), and its gardens. Few of the houses in Borth had front lawns, and we always grew the sweetest smelling dianthus (pinks) which made people stop and stare and catch the scent. A wonderful pathway of pebbles led up to the front door, laid by the captain's family, with a heart outlined in white stones. This heart seemed to inspire the strangest stories. I heard that there was a pirate buried beneath it, who made his presence felt! Highly unlikely I suspect, as it was my Aunty Get's artistic interests that inspired it. Long walls of heavy slate extended to the gate. It was possible to see the dents where the Evans children played a game with cherry stones and chicken bones.

Even in my childhood I played games there with the children of our summer visitors (to whom we rented out half the house). There were so many glorious summer afternoons on that lawn as we sat and chatted with a stream of visitors. My mother's lovely pastel sketches captured those idyllic days of summer. As noted, winters were windy and rainy, but only once do I remember the drama of snow. In the winter of 1978 there was so heavy a fall of snow that the wind blew it right up to our roof and we had to be dug out of our front door by lifeboat men.

It was strange that we seemed to live a life of two halves. Summers full of laughter and people, and winters were empty when I mainly had the company of old folk.

The missing gap – the Public Hall

Next door to Saxatile used to be the Public Hall, the hub of village life. It used to host a vast variety of community events – a small village eisteddfod, dramas by local groups, Sunday night concerts, dances and billiards. When I was a teenager I used to think the dances were great fun. I learnt to twist and jive, but some of the village's young men left a lot to be desired. On one occasion a bachelor postman wandered in with his dog. When he was asked why he had brought his dog, he replied, 'for bloody company, man'! There was a boy from Dol-y-Bont whose only conversation was, 'Have you had the flu this winter?' Then there was the odd dashing fellow who tried to get a passionate embrace as part of the usual doorstep goodnight kiss. The chat-up line I most enjoyed was, 'You are a challenge to a full-bloodied Celt'. It did not work, mainly because his beard stank of cigarettes!

If my girlfriends and I had only been more adventurous, we might have wandered up to the local caravan site for entertainment. But, it was something we just didn't do. The caravans had spoilt the trade for renting out village houses as summer lets. We found our excitement by promenading up and down the sea wall, trying to attract a little male attention, or playing bingo in the newly-opened bingo hall. I actually had to confess such decadence to my mother when I won a set of apostle spoons!

The Libanus chapel, where we worshipped, was a copious building with a big 'sêt fawr' for the deacons. A stream of theology academics from the university at Aberystwyth came to preach, and we were expected to take our turn in providing the visiting preachers with a hearty lunch. At the back of the chapel was a vestry which held social activities, with its own eisteddfod, dramas and talks. Ironically, my grandmother remembered the chapel being built, and later having a fall there because the maid did not look after her properly when they went to look at the builders at work.

An odd quirk of fate is that Libanus has had a new lease of life as a bijou cinema and restaurant which serves splendid food.

Schools

Peter was a little puzzled that there had been a handsome primary school opposite Ardwyn. 'Why didn't you go there?'

'Aunty Get had taught at the top school. All good Methodists went to the top school. No way would we go to an Anglican school! I know it seems a little silly when we had to walk right from the centre of the village up that very steep hill, but there was a reward halfway up the hill; we could to buy broken biscuits for a penny a bag at Castle Stores.'

My only memory of my first years at school was singing a lullaby to my doll at a concert and, halfway through the music, realising to my horror I was swinging up her upside down! I made an effort to knit a scarf for my teddy bear, and for some reason attempted to dance a Highland jig over a pair of pokers in front of the fireplace.

When I moved up to the next two classes, Mr Stevens and Mr James put my lively imagination to better use. The whole primary school only had 50 pupils, divided into three classrooms, so it was quite a challenge for teachers as they frequently had several separate lessons for the different age groups going on in the one classroom. Mr James, the headmaster, worked hard to get us through the Eleven Plus (then known as the Scholarship), giving extra classes after school. In my year I was the only one out of four pupils to pass, much to my mother's relief. She celebrated by buying me every single item on the school uniform list, including a heavy green winter coat and green serge knickers, complete with pocket. It took me a long time after I left school for me to wear green again.

Grammar school was an adventure, as it meant catching a double-decker bus to travel to Aberystwyth. Adapting to the big school was complicated for me, as I sprouted up to being five foot eight inches tall and was rather bosomy at 11 years old, which only increased my shyness and self-consciousness. Curiously, we were segregated, as on the school bus boys sat upstairs and girls downstairs. In classrooms boys and girls never sat together at the double desks, and there were separate playgrounds for us. In the sixth form there was a girls' prefect room and a boys' prefect room. Even more amazing was the fact that the staffrooms were split up for men and women too, so frequently there were long conversations on stairways between the male and female teachers, as that was the only place they could meet!

By today's standards it was a small secondary school of only 600 pupils. It followed the 1950s procedure of being able to choose between sciences and arts subjects in the third year (now Year 9). Luckily, I chose history and geography, both of which were taught by two gifted teachers. Noel Butler, the history teacher, had laughing dark eyes and a genuine passion for his subject and was a great support to me when my father died when I was 14 years old. The geography master, Roy James, was a colourful character, with a bellowing voice and a limp. He had been in the army during the war and travelled his way around Britain, which meant that he had a knack of bringing Ordnance Survey maps to life because he seemed to have been everywhere with the army.

Ironically, considering my creative interests, I found little inspiration in my English classes. We spent our A level classes listening to an elderly teacher reading from his university notes. It was what we might consider the extra-curricular activities which really shaped me. I thoroughly enjoyed a formal debating class on the issues of the day. I was developing my passion for public speaking. We had an eisteddfod which was run competitively across house teams in the splendour of the King's Hall in Aberystwyth. The eisteddfod got me writing prose at least, even if poetry was beyond me. I had my moment of glory by winning the best play in the drama festival held at the Little Theatre. Best of all, it was adjudicated by a local playwright. What an honour!

Sadly, the King's Hall and the Little Theatre have long since gone.

Defences

Peter and I went back to the beach mindful of what the girl in the café, where we had stopped for coffee, had said. She had told us about future plans for Borth. It's obvious how vulnerable the beach and the village are. A complicated coastal defence scheme was due to go ahead in 2011 with the help of Welsh Assembly and European money. It's a scheme that's difficult to envisage. What effect would it have on Borth in the future?

The coastal defence system involved building of rock groynes and breakwaters, moving shingle and sand to reinforce the beach, and building a multi-purpose barrier reef to help extend the beach and alter the pattern of waves to improve its 'surfability'. Quite mind-boggling! As it happens, Prince Charles surfed on Borth beach when he was a student at UCW, Aberystwyth. He even left a footprint on some wet cement as he left the beach. It's still there!

When Peter and I returned in 2019, we found much had changed with the coming of the defences. The beach had actually shrunk and large boulders were scattered everywhere. There was no more glorious stretches of golden sand reaching out for great distances. An obvious advantage is that the stumps of the 'submerged forest' made more regular appearances. And, during the storms of 2014, the beach had been littered with large aged tree trunks.

Controversy still rages about just how damaging climate change will be for the future of the village.

The way to adventure

Back to the railway station and there, glittering before us, was the line leading far away in the distance towards my big adventure when I was 11 years old. I still feel a quiver of excitement at the memory of it. I went to London on my own on the Cambrian Express! What splendour! My mother had actually given me enough money to buy a lunch of three courses in the dining car at a proper table covered with a fine white tablecloth. Then, the frenzied hunt at Euston station for my Aunty Chris, my father's sister, but what pleasures she was to open up for me on my stay with her. There was Frankie Howerd as Bottom in *A Midsummer Night's Dream* at the Old Vic, the treasures of the paintings at the Dulwich Art Gallery, all those royal palaces, and trips up and down the Thames. So began a life-changing experience. Not a year has passed since without my visiting London art galleries or theatres, that is until Covid frightened me out of London.

My Aunty Chris was a remarkable woman who financed herself through university by chamber maiding, and eventually learned ten languages which took her to France and Chile and eventually to work for the UN in Geneva and New York. What an inspiration! What a world she opened up to a shy Welsh girl! There were travels to Switzerland and France with her during my teens, and amazingly it meant that I developed the courage to set out alone for five years of excitement in a new life in the Maritimes, Canada.

University was important in my father's family. My father had put up a fierce fight to get to university to do an agricultural economics degree by doing his initial qualifications by correspondence course. He had actually left school at 13 to work on a farm, and only decided to work his way into university in his latter teens. So I had a rich inheritance from both my parents!

In 1984, when my mother moved from Saxatile to join me in East Anglia, we began to sort out the treasures of the old home. The memories of the days of the master mariners slowly began to seep back, and I gradually began to piece together the amazing lives of my great-grandparents, the captain and his lady.

PART II
The Captain's Life

CHAPTER 1

That portrait of
the captain and his wife

THE CAPTAIN AND his lady stand erect in a portrait I know so well. The presence of master mariner John Evans and his wife was a dominating force in the family's life in Saxatile. This portrait hung over a black marble fireplace in the room we called the big room. It was a gigantic and startling picture.

As a teenager I found it alarming, not only because of its physical enormity but because the couple seemed the personification of Victorian rectitude, two disciplinarians who could stand no nonsense. The photograph would have made a fine cover for a melodrama full of secrets. Yet, all I could find was evidence of grim Methodism. Weighty black Bibles were everywhere. It was clear that the worthy captain would never go to sea without his Bible in his cabin. The only 'lighter' work was his well-thumbed Welsh version of *Pilgrim's Progress*. Unfortunately, the only letter of theirs we ever found was to their three daughters when the captain and Sarah were away at sea. It reminded the girls to milk the cows and to read their Bible.

I definitely felt that the couple were staring down at me disapprovingly – I was unnerved. Even as an adult, I still felt inadequate in front of them. Perhaps, if I had looked more closely, I might have noticed the suggestion of a smile lurking beneath the captain's luxuriant whiskers. Yet I don't think he

Captain John Evans and his wife.

would have approved of me at all. After all, I did try to sell that portrait. Let me tell you the story behind it.

My mother and I decided to sell Saxatile in 1984. I had left the village in 1964 after my days at the university in Aberystwyth. I felt that the time had come for my mother to join me in the home that I had made for myself in East Anglia. It was a difficult time. Which of the house's treasures were we take with us? Mostly, Mum and I agreed what to take, but I was determined to sell that portrait. Secretly, I agreed to sell it to an antique shop in Aberystwyth which could sell it to some interior decorator with fancy ideas. The captain's ghost must have known what I was up to, for my mother found out. Her redhead temper got the better of her.

'Get your coat on. We're going to get the bus into Aber to sort this out immediately. How could you be so disrespectful?'

We were not greeted warmly by the antique shop owner. We had to negotiate to buy it back. He was not pleased, but he did not argue with my mother. Few people argued with my mother when she was angry.

So, after all, the portrait made the journey to Brightlingsea. Ironically, in the confusion of unloading the furniture van, it was shoved into a cupboard under the stairs. The move was such a nightmare, as the removal men had to contend with so much heavy oak furniture. Mum never mentioned the painting again, and now it's banished to the attic where nobody sees it.

Chapter 2

Saxatile – the captain's house

It was not easy parting with the old captain's house. Saxatile was one of the two oldest houses in Borth, but we knew in our heart of hearts that my mother could not go on living there alone. Old houses need a special kind of cherishing, especially ones by the sea, and poor old Saxatile suffered terribly from damp if left unoccupied for any length of time. My mother was finding it all too much to keep up with the repairs needed. I'm grateful that I took her away before it became too much of a problem for her.

The name of the house was spelt in brass letters nailed onto a wooden plaque. It seems to have been the name that the Evans family gave the house in the 1870s. Aunty Get always used to tell me the name was Greek, and referred to stones and rocks. It was a name that intrigued visitors. So many Borth houses had names that were either the name of a ship, or the names of places visited on a voyage.

Above the front door was a fanlight that had panes of purple and amber glass which threw beams of colour on the stairs carpet when the door was open on a sunny day. I used to love sitting on the stairs in the oak-panelled hallway, holding up my hand and watching the blotches of purple and amber throw patterns of light across my knuckles.

There was a sitting room, an enormous dining room, a kitchen, a scullery and four bedrooms. After we moved in, a large bathroom took the place of the back bedroom. The house was full of enormous oak furniture and it was possible to fill the big room with an eight-foot by eight-foot dresser, a gigantic hanging press, a sideboard with a marble top, six lovely sabre-backed chairs, and a massive mahogany table which seated eight and wobbled on a splendid pedestal.

I often wondered if an Uppingham schoolboy once lodged there, for one of the boys once described staying in a house in Borth, 'with its stone kitchen floor, polished wainscoting and oak furniture, its walls hung with prints of Nonconformist worthies and its kitchen dresser with ranks of ancestral crockery'. It certainly sounds a little like Saxatile.

Unusually for Borth, and as noted already, there were gardens at the front and back of the house. The captain's family grew vegetables in the back garden and kept a cow. It also seems more than likely that, like many houses in the village, Saxatile kept up the Cardiganshire tradition of keeping a pig. The village was never free of the smell of manure. In fact, a report in 1873 gave the village a very unattractive description. It said there were 200 houses, only 70 of which had privies.

My memories of our back garden were more romantic! Grandma said that rose bushes were planted and named after each of the captain's children. And how could I forget the strawberries, which Aunty Get always served with cream from a strawberry patterned jug and sugar bowl? We would sit in the kitchen feasting on the sweet fruit under a large print of Millais' *Cherry Ripe* which I always thought was so picturesque.

There was a privy in the back garden surrounded by Aunty Jane's pink cabbage roses. As noted, a bathroom appeared in the 1950s when we moved in. (I had to endure the humiliation of having to bathe in a neighbour's house across the road for the first two years that we lived in Saxatile.) There was a vast cellar that ran under the house, but it was for coal, not wine! A lean-to shed sheltered the boiler and tin baths for washing and, of course, the mangle. There was even a large slab of stone in the garden where the water could be beaten out of the washing.

At the bottom of the garden was the railway line, beyond which we could see St Matthew's church, a farm, the peat bogs and the hills which glowed purple, green or blue according to the changing light. Sometimes they were snow covered. Occasionally, wildlife from Cors Fochno would come into the garden. I remember opening the curtains one morning to find a peregrine falcon staring back at me!

I don't remember being told about 'hen wrach ddu y figin' (the old black witch of the bog), but my grandmother certainly believed in witches. I remember her warning me about a woman who had a hare in her house. With the knowledge I now have of folklore, I realise what she was trying to say. She was hinting that the woman was a witch. A hare is a well-known Celtic witch's familiar. Boudica was said to have gone into battle with a hare at her feet. There were even tales in Borth of black goblins which came out of coffins; 'rheibio' (a curse) was always a real danger and people often spoke of 'knockers' underground in the lead mines up in the hills.

The more we tried to list the contents of the house, the more the memories came flooding back. It certainly seemed that the captain lived in some style compared with other captains in the village. It's odd that he doesn't seem to have brought home many treasures from his trips aboard. His children did at least have the fun of a parrot and a tortoise, which must have come from some exotic port. The tortoise had a bad habit of hibernating under a corner of the carpet in the dining room, and visitors were continually warned of his presence or there could be a nasty crunch.

CHAPTER 3

The family treasures

As WELL AS many childhood memories, there were some splendid treasures to take with us when my mother left Borth. They were not just interesting antiques but historical mementoes of the great age of sail in Cardigan Bay.

Like many eager young sea captains, Captain Evans had a portrait of his first ship painted. Ship portraits go back a long way. They first began with early maps from the fifteenth to the seventeenth centuries, when the seas on the maps were usually decorated with drawings of small ships. Gradually, traders began to ask that their individual ships be drawn. Joseph Roux (1725–93) of Marseille was one of the first people to draw ships on commission and, as the business grew, more draftsmen were required.

By the nineteenth century there were artists sitting waiting on the pierhead, with the landscape of the port already blocked in, so only the ship needed to be added! Many of these were produced almost like on a conveyer belt, and can really only be thought of as folk art. But, the paintings that were signed and dated deserved to be treated like works of art. Sadly, as Danish maritime artist Antonio Jacobsen said, 'No more than a painted ship about a painted ocean remains of that great merchant fleet that they created.'

It was certainly a sad truth about those Welsh ships that traded all over the world. Many local families had ships' pictures, but we were especially proud of our two paintings, especially as I was able to find out their family significance.

Sarah

The *Sarah* was Captain Evans' first ship as master, when he was 34 years old. The 106-ton schooner was named after his wife. Like so many other vessels of this period, it traded along the Mediterranean, Adriatic and Black seas, Holland and Belgium, but mainly around the Welsh coast from Newport to Liverpool. The crew were all Borth men for the six years of its voyages between 1858 and 1864, and often included two apprentices, usually about 16 years old. Its early voyages were bedevilled by arguments between John Evans and first mate David Rees. In fact, on the first voyage in 1858, David Rees was master and John Evans was mate, but then they appeared to have changed roles.

I'm afraid that John Evans was a little smug about this. He wrote to the authorities saying: 'With reference to the agreement being signed by me, I beg to state that the former master David Rees had neglected to do so, and when I took charge of the vessel myself I thought it my duty to supply the omission.' It's interesting to note that on future occasions he was not so careful about his paperwork to the authorities.

Sadly, we have no detailed description of *Sarah*'s last adventure. On 9 April 1864 she was lost in the Bay of Biscay, no doubt in one of the terrible storms that are a feature of that part of the world. Fortunately, every member of the crew was saved, so Captain John Evans lived to sail other ships.

Sarah and Mary

Our beautiful painting of the *Sarah and Mary* had always been assumed by us to be my great-grandfather's ship named after my grandmother. This was wrong. Research by Barbara Walker of Derwenlas found out the truth. It turns out that, in fact, the *Sarah and Mary* was the first ship that shipbuilder Rowland Evans had built in Derwenlas, and it was named after his two daughters. The link with our family had been that both John Evans the elder and John Evans the younger of Cwmcethin (the worthy captain's grandfather and father) had served as masters aboard her. In fact, John Evans the elder had bought 16 shares in the new vessel. It was a schooner of 76 tons.

Barbara researched the ship's history in 2015 for a display of historic paintings at the National Eisteddfod in Montgomeryshire. She found a crew list from 1866, which mentions that the managing owner was John Evans of Morben (Rowland Evans' son) and that the crew included two Borth men. The crew worked all kinds of cargoes, such as moving salt from London to Poole, calling at Ellesmere Port, being laid up at Caernarfon; then going on to Aberdyfi for limestone, then to Greenock for oak bark, and then to Ardrossan for ballast and then on to collect pig iron. After many years of trading around the British coast, the *Sarah and Mary* was converted into a storage hulk, probably for coal, in 1914. By 1920 the ship had disintegrated in Falmouth dock.

It's a remarkably fine painting which appears to have been painted by Dutchman Dirk Antoon Teupken (1828–59). He was a painter and shopkeeper for writing and drawing supplies, and lived all his life in Amsterdam and was well known for his ships' portraits.

How did our family come to own the painting? It may have been sold to the Evans family when the Morben yard was sold. It certainly stands out as a far more polished work among the more primitive paintings of other Borth and Aberystwyth ships.

However, the mystery is why there is no portrait of the ship, the *Rowland Evans*.

*

These family treasures were helpful in tracking down the family history. I was not enthusiastic about prowling my way through all those Evanses. I needed help, and I was extremely grateful to my cousin Roy Williams and my friend Val Johnson who gave me information to help me understand the tools that family historians use, such as parish records, birth/marriage/death certificates, census returns, and inscriptions in graveyards. There were at times such a tangle of Evanses, Joneses and Lloyds that I nearly lost heart. Independent researcher Eirionedd Baskerville's meticulous research through parish records began eventually to make sense of my family tree.

Captain John Evans married into farming stock. It was hard to find his wife Sarah at first. Trying to trace maiden names for the wives of these nautical families was a nightmare. It was difficult enough trying to sort out the countless John Evanses, but Sarah's maiden name was that other popular Welsh surname – Jones!

I had tried to discover the maiden name of John Evans' bride, Sarah. But the answer had been with us all the time. We had a fine sampler, made by a Mary Jones, aged 15 in 1835, and two examples of Berlin wool work embroidery, made by a Margaret Jones, aged 13 in 1849. As might be expected, the sampler had a suitably religious hymn worked upon it.

Take my poor heart just as it is,
Set up there in thy throne
So shall I love thee above all
And live to thee alone.

So, there it was. This was a clue to John Evans' bride's name! It was Jones, as it was the only surname mentioned on the samplers hanging in the house.

Mary's work was a traditional sampler, showing different kind of stitches and using the letters of the alphabet, flowers and an abstract design. Margaret's two pictures of Berlin wool work used cross and tent stitches to depict a realistic design. The designs had been drawn on squared paper first so that they could be worked on canvas. The wools used were very bright colours. As a child I loved the Biblical scene, with the wonderful red tablecloth which seemed almost to protrude from the frame.

The next step was to find where Sarah Jones came from. I remembered my grandmother and great-aunts referring to the white tea service at the bottom of the corner cupboard as Grandma Rhiwlas' wedding service (Rhiwlas was a well-known local farm). The tea service was considered so grand, with its turquoise stones and white porcelain, that it never left the corner cupboard.

So she was a farmer's daughter, and no doubt that was where the money came from when times were hard. It was finally their wedding certificate that confirmed her name. Another treasure in the corner cupboard was a sail smoother, which had been there for many years without our knowing what purpose it served. Ironically, it was a neighbour of ours in East Anglia who explained what it was. Most sail smoothers were functional, as they were intended to rub down the seams of sails and smooth out the stitches. This one was special. It seemed to have the look of a love token, for it had hearts carved into the side, and the names William Hughes and Borth on the front. It had a beautifully carved ropework on the handle and was a lovely example of this kind of work. It must have helped the young sailor endure long hours at sea.

In the corner cupboard also was a lovely engraved glass of Captain A. Lloyd's 1865 schooner, the *Martha Lloyd*. This was built in Aberdyfi and owned by more than one Borth family. Eventually, it was wrecked off the coast of Holland. It was not until I tried to piece together my family tree that I realised the connection between the Evans family and the Lloyd family. John Evans' sister, Elizabeth, married Thomas Lloyd on 27

November 1863. He was a mariner, who in time became a master mariner, and he and his family of five children lived with Mary Evans, their grandmother, in Cwmcethin. The Lloyds were an amazing family of mariners going back to the 1700s and continued to play a major role in maritime life into the twentieth century.

CHAPTER 4

Captain John Evans' early life

So WHAT WAS the captain's early life like? Well, he was brought up in a rather splendid house called Cwmcethin in the hamlet of Glan-y-wern. The house had some land and a stream, and was used as a smallholding.

His grandfather Captain Morgan John Evans' life had also been bound to the sea. His grave can be found in the graveyard of Llanfihangel Genau'r Glyn where it records that he died on 14 September 1808 at the age of 71. He appears among the master mariners in the *Welsh Mariners Index*. It is clear that he was the founder of the family's fortunes.

His father John Evans is buried there too, with his wife. We know that he was born in 1792 and died aged 61 in 1853. The parish records note that he married a Mary Benjamin in 1824 and lived at Cwmcethin. They had three children, John, Jane and Elizabeth. Ceredigion Archives record him as the master of the *Sarah and Mary*.

I find it strange that there is very little mention of Mary by the three sisters at Saxatile.

Mary may have looked stern, but she seems to be a kind person with a strong personality. Her portrait is to be seen in the photograph section.

We get an interesting glimpse of life at Cwmcethin from the census returns of 1851 to 1881. In 1851, Mary has her parents and her two daughters living with her, while her husband

and son are probably at sea. By the next census in 1861 she has been widowed and her son has married and moved to his new home at Saxatile. Mary had been left with only £25, as her husband died intestate. Mary's father became a ship's carpenter to try to increase the family's income.

By 1871 Mary's father has died and her daughter and husband, mariner Thomas Lloyd, and their three children under five, are living with her. Mary is referred to as a 'farmer' now. Maybe she had a few pigs and a cow. By the 1881 census Thomas Lloyd is a master mariner, so there is an increase in household income and only two children are at home.

Mary lived to the grand old age of 91 (according to the parish burial record) or 92 (according to her gravestone). Her striking photograph was taken by famous photographer John Thomas (1838–1905). There she sits, solidly on a chair beside her front door. She looks like a capable, hard-working person with her apron, shawl and bonnet. This is obviously someone who worked hard all her life.

*

So how did her son, our Captain John Evans, start his life as a mariner? The first thing he would need to have done was to learn English. There was a choice of two primary schools in the village – the British School in Upper Borth for Nonconformists, and the National School in the centre of the village for Anglicans. As a Methodist, it was inevitable that he would go to the Upper Borth school. Here he would have gained a reasonable standard of literacy and fluency in English that made it possible for him to gain a captain's ticket and sail the world. The real practical knowledge for a master mariner, however, was gained from classes in navigation at private homes. If you went to private classes it would cost you three pence a week. Three pence well spent, considering the opportunities it opened up. It's not impossible that he might have gone to a lady for these lessons. Why else does a tiny lady appear in one of those famous photographs of captains taken by John Thomas? The most famous female teacher of navigation in Cardiganshire was Sarah Jane Rees (1839–1916) of Llangrannog.

Working as a young apprentice on ships would mean starting off as a second mate. Then promotion to first mate, who had to understand how to manage the sails in all kinds of weather. This meant going up the highest rigging on the ship in very dangerous conditions. The first mate also had to understand how to load various cargoes. It was never the easiest of jobs, for there were no derricks then, so the cargo had to be pulled along on a series of planks. No wonder there was an eagerness to be promoted, as so much of the work in the lower ranks was incredibly physical and exhausting. Older men found it unbearable.

John Evans applied for a captain's ticket in Dublin. To achieve this he needed to be able to keep his ship in good order and take it into dry dock when necessary. He would also need to know how to cope with fires and storms, collisions and sinkings. There were many prevailing winds and currents on the world trade routes, and he would need to understand tides, use maps and nautical instruments. A captain had a legal obligation to keep a log book regularly. Then there was dealing with business arrangements, hiring and paying crews, and bills for the handling of cargo. Much of this knowledge was gained during the hurly-burly of life at sea.

John Evans' imposing build must have been sufficient to show his authority over the crew. He did have a weakness – he hated paperwork, something which was to get him into trouble with the authorities. Yet, he could be surprisingly gentle when younger members of the crew were sick.

*

John married 20-year-old Sarah Jones, as custom decreed, at her church in Llanfihangel Genau'r Glyn, Llandre, an Anglican church rather than a Nonconformist chapel. (However, for the rest of her life she was very much a 'chapel' person.) John and Sarah's marriage certificate gave several useful pieces of information. They were married on 29 March 1854. He was 36 and they then moved to a house called Morfa, Borth.

Sarah's family in the 1851 Census		
Name	Age	Occupation / Relationship
William Jones	66	Farmer
Jane Jones	56	Farmer's Wife
Jane Jones	28	Farmer's Daughter
David Jones	20	Farmer's Son
Sarah Jones	17	Farmer's Daughter
Margaret Jones	15	Farmer's Daughter
Thomas Pryse*	5	Grandson

(*Thomas Pryse, Sarah's nephew, was later to sail frequently with his uncle on the *Rowland Evans*.)

Prior to her marriage, and following local custom, Sarah would have gathered together clothes, linen and crockery for her new life. Her husband, as a mariner, would have made a model of a fully-rigged ship to show his method of earning his living. Four mariners would have carried the model ship to the church in the wedding procession from Borth to Llandre.

Sarah's daughters always spoke of her gently, as though she needed protection. They treated her royally. Sarah certainly had a queenly air about her, with her fine lace cap and gold earrings. She had little in common with the raucous cockle women of Borth who were known to smoke pipes and drink heavily.

Like many women at that time, she lost her first-born

child. In the graveyard of Llanfihangel Genau'r Glyn is a little tombstone engraved: 'Sacred to the memory of John, son of John and Mary Evans, Morfa, Borth, born 8 February 1857, died March 1857.' Confusingly, the name for the mother is given as Mary. Infant mortality was frequent at this time.

This inscription gives us a clue as to the problem of when the Evans family actually moved into Saxatile. The obvious date would be immediately after John and Sarah's wedding in 1854. However, all references mention their home, up until the 1870s, as being called Morfa. A letter that my father wrote to St Fagans National Museum of History suggests that Saxatile was formerly known as Morfa – as already noted it was one of the two oldest houses in Borth. It seems that, sometime in the late 1870s, they decided to change the name of the house and call it Saxatile.

CHAPTER 5

The captain's children

THE CAPTAIN AND Sarah had four surviving children, three girls and one boy.

Jane

Jane, the eldest of the girls, was the practical one and loved the vegetable garden at the back of the house. I remember her racing up and down stairs, carrying the old-fashioned stoneware hot water bottles to keep the beds aired. At one time she was a parlour maid. She had remarkably long thin legs, rather like a grasshopper. She and my father would argue about the best way to plant vegetables. He knew the scientific theory; she had the best practical experience. Later she was the landlady when, after her parents' death, Saxatile became a lodging house.

Sarah Mary

Sarah Mary, nicknamed Sal, the middle daughter, was a lady of fixed opinions who was a stickler for going to chapel three times on a Sunday. She always dressed as sprucely as possible; Sunday best always included scented gloves and elaborate hats. She was the only daughter to marry, perhaps as she was the only one with a knack for flirtation. I remember, even in her 90s, her receiving a gentleman caller who remembered her fondly.

In 1914, as a middle-aged woman, she married a wealthy man, W.T. Lewis, who owned a splendid general store called London House. Unfortunately, W.T. preferred to act out his role as a magistrate, or play billiards and gamble on the stock exchange rather than conduct his shop's business. As well as being a lazy shopkeeper, he took bad advice from his bank manager and invested in stocks and shares that slumped, the most notorious being shares in Baku oil fields just as the Russian Revolution broke out. He had originally owned five houses, but by the time he was an old man he only owned Ardwyn.

His one moment of glory was the prospect of a visit from Lloyd George, the Prime Minister. But even that did not happen, for the great man sent his apologies and a signed photograph instead!

Sarah Mary was his second wife and she kept his business going and cared for the children of his first marriage, Alfie and my mother. She had the splendid name of Sarah Vivienne Gwynora.

The only memory my mother had of her own mother was when she was four years old, gazing at her mother's corpse laying in her coffin, looking incredibly beautiful with her red hair spread over her shoulders and engulfed in a sheaf of arum lilies. My mother was lucky enough to inherit that glorious red hair, but I did not.

What a romantic vision she seemed but, later in my life, I did inherit something from my grandmother which was a horrible shock. When I was 45 I got breast cancer which had been my grandmother's fatal illness. I was fortunate that my illness was diagnosed early and I only had to have radiotherapy, but it was nevertheless something which was to change my life.

Actually my mother, Gwynora, gave all her affection and respect to her stepmother. She knew little of her own mother, and it was obvious that Sarah Mary was worthy of respect. The shop became a prosperous endeavour and household affairs were conducted with remarkable efficiency when Sarah Mary was in charge. London House was quite a challenge, for it was a vast barracks of a place and needed the assistance of a washerwoman to keep all the household linen in order, which must have been quite an exhausting task as everything had to be washed and dried by hand.

My mother was sent as an eight-year-old boarder to Dr Williams' School in Dolgellau. She suffered dreadful bouts of homesickness. She remembered crying in the cloakroom and one of the day girls bringing her a posy of flowers. Most of all, she resented having to leave her tomboy ways behind her – no more fishing in rock pools or riding bikes.

She was more of a tomboy than me as a child. She would love making sandcastles and get thoroughly damp and sandy. On one occasion she turned up to her piano lesson, after one of these expeditions, looking thoroughly dishevelled. Her piano teacher said nothing but sent her home with a note. She was totally unaware of what it said. My grandmother's face darkened as she read, 'Gwynora turned up to her piano lesson like this.' One glance at the ragamuffin in front of her was enough for Grandma. It was a hairbrush across the bottom that night for my mother.

My mother could always find a hideaway when she was in real trouble, for there were fishing boats on the beach and she could always persuade someone to take her out on a fishing trip. Another of her passions was her bike. On one occasion she was so eager to see her friend Muriel that she cycled right into the sitting room and into the middle of their afternoon tea!

Her brother Alfie was born with an arm only to the elbow. He was what they used to call in the old days 'backward'. He was a familiar sight in the village, delivering bread in a funny little trolley that went from house to house. Sarah Mary was very protective of him, even during his more eccentric moments; for example, the occasion when he wandered upstairs uninvited into an old lady's attic to look for wheels when one fell off his trolley!

Margaretta (Get)

Aunty Get, the youngest daughter, was plain and short-sighted, but she was a sweet person and everybody who knew her loved her dearly. She was a well-respected school teacher at the primary school in Upper Borth. She would go up and down the hill four times a day, as she would go home for lunch.

She took trouble to dress very smartly, as her colleagues dressed with lot of jewellery. Belts were very important.

She was a warm and loving person and the one most interested in the world outside the village. She was the keenest to keep in touch with her brother William when he left home. They were the two with a liveliest sense of humour, and had odd nicknames for each other. He was Rex and she was Madge. She was eager to try out any new hobby that came into fashion, including wood carving, leather tooling, sketching and riding a bicycle. She even rode her bicycle on a visit to Kenilworth. Her collection of postcards showed an interest in the world, especially during the First World War when she organised several charitable events for refugees, even for Russian families, which stirred up a great deal of sympathy.

William

The family member I never knew, sadly, was William, who went to sea like his father. His sea-going experiences were mainly on steamships. His first voyage was on his father's ship, the *Rowland Evans*. The crew lists show him sailing on the same ship in 1876 as a bosun. Obviously, this was a step in the direction of his getting a master's ticket. William was very different from his father. He was a charmer, a dandy and a man of the world who always wore a diamond ring on his little finger. All his life was dedicated to steamships. As master of his own ship, he made his home in South Shields. The postcards he sent 'Madge' came from as far afield as Buenos Aires, Venice, Hamburg, Karachi and Mobile.

Surname	Forename	Place of Birth	Year of Birth	CC or Cs No.	Died/Pens.
EVANS	William	Borth	1858	09928	
Reg.Ticket	**Capacities**	**County of Birth**	**Kew Ref.**		
	om81 Mfa84	CGN	122/79		
1m/62328/Brazilian/1888. Master of the *Jerseymoor, Castlemoor, Raithmoor* & *Elmmoor* from 1895–1912. C/98429/Sydney Reid/1916–21. C/136157/Western Valleys/1912–14. Vessel broken in two, pilot in charge. C/143969/Frederick Cleaves/1925–6. (LCR Ms:18569/11)					

There is so much I would like to have known about him. Unfortunately, I have lost contact with his side of the family. His first wife was a rare beauty who knew how to silence her husband. Hearing him shouting at the docks, she'd glance at him and say, 'Do you really have to shout so, William.' Unusually, their daughter Myfi was educated at a convent and became a very fashionable young woman with all the airs of a flapper about town. Young Ivor, their son, seems to have had a Little Lord Fauntleroy air about him in the only photograph we have of him (see photograph section).

The courtship of his second wife stunned his sisters, as she was a widow who lived in Borth. Nobody knew how they had met up in South Shields. She was always referred to as 'that woman'! I never quite knew why, but I think it might have been suspected that she was chasing William for his money.

The family story that has always intrigued me most, however, is how he came to be in St Petersburg during the 1917 revolution and found a silver cigarette case lying in the gutter. My mother was lucky enough to inherit that cigarette case. He certainly had spirit, for he was still commanding a ship in his 70s. Our dreams of the cigarette case being a Fabergé were quickly eliminated after a visit to Sotheby's. Apparently, according to the experts, it was machine-made and the owner's jewelled initial which should have hung from the case's centre was missing. Even though they said it was machine-made, I still found it romantic, as there was a rather lovely engraving of three horses pulling a vehicle known as a troika in Russia.

CHAPTER 6

Borth – a village
of master mariners

So what was it like to live in a village famous its master mariners? Borth has beautiful views of Cardigan Bay, but it was an unlikely village for sailors as it had no proper harbour. Fishing in small boats was possible, but not the launching of large ships. As Terry Davies, the village's most knowledgeable historian, has written, 'Borth's history reveals a resourceful people living in unimaginable cottages, built precariously on an exposed coastal shingle beach, flanked on one side by a gale-lashed storm beach and on the other by the marshland of Cors Fochno.' Borth was to produce many master mariners who sailed around the world; they probably spent more time at sea than they did in their own homes.

The great admirer of the county's commercial maritime history, David Jenkins, says of our own age, 'Cardiganshire, one of the great nurseries of seamen in the British Isles, has turned its back on the sea,' meaning that commercial shipping in this area has now come to end. Cardiganshire men certainly continued to serve in the Merchant Navy and Royal Navy during both world wars, as seen on First and Second World War memorials. However, they do not appear in modern nautical history.

Photographer John Thomas took some remarkable group photographs of these adventurous and successful Borth sea

John Thomas' photograph of Borth sea captains in 1890.
© National Library of Wales

captains in 1890. Then there were well over 40 master mariners in the village and what colourful characters they all were, sporting an amazing array of facial hair and hats! Some wore a full three-piece suit with a pocket watch chain and bowler hat; some wore jackets and workmen's caps, and others wore stout fisherman's jerseys.

In one photograph my great-grandfather Captain John Evans stands proudly in the back row (second man on the left). The photographer has tried to label the captains by the names of their ships. John Evans looks an imposingly tall man, with a fine set of whiskers and an unlikely tweed hat. Judging by the way he stands, this is a man of great independence of spirit, yet 1890 was to prove to be one of the most humiliating years of his life, as we shall see later. There is also something rather shabby about him, a hint of the mystery which was to destroy his life.

Captain Hugh Hughes stands at his left, looking the most dapper of the captains, complete with cane, stiff collar and three-piece suit with flyaway jacket. He smokes a pipe and looks very proud, for he owns several properties. He is one of

a clan of over 50 men from the Hughes family who went to sea
– 20 of whom were master mariners.

Towards the end of the back row is a man with a very
brown face and a monkey-like fringe of a beard. This is
Captain David Rees, who was fully aware of Captain Evans'
strength of character as a young man, for he had struggled
to be captain of the schooner *Sarah* with him, and lost. He
managed, however, to have a full career at sea.

His son, Thomas Rees, began his career at 14 years old,
and worked for the Hough & Coast Line, and stayed at sea
until he was 59 years old, mainly trading between London
and Liverpool. He became wealthy enough to import timber
from North America to build a fine house called Arequipa in
Borth, and could afford to send his son to Shrewsbury School.
His obituary spoke of him being 'a lofty-minded man, quiet,
modest and reliable and highly respected'. This could also
easily be a description of his daughter Dilys, a lovely lady who
was my Sunday school teacher.

In the front row sits David Hughes (with a very full beard),
who opened the Friendship Inn in Borth. All these men sailed
some very impressive ships. The earnest looking Richard Jones
(back row, fourth left) seems to have sailed his brigantine
Charlotte to many of the places sailed to by Captain Evans, like
South America and the West Indies. John Hughes (front row,
third right) wears a nosegay, and sailed the 74-ton schooner
Lorne, alternating command of it with his father. Sharing a
ship among family members seemed to be a frequent feature
of Borth master mariners.

It's interesting that being a sea captain didn't necessarily
mean that a man might live a life of prosperity. It depended on
the wealth of the cargoes that the ship carried. The hats seem
to give it away as to the man's status. The capped men even
looked ill-fed but the gentlemen in bowlers have an affluent air
about them, with their pocket watch chains and silk cravats.

The development of Borth

These men grew up in a village that mainly consisted of simple cottages. The tithe map of 1845 showed that Borth was divided in two; one section on a shingle bank known as Morfa, and the other on sloping ground known as Upper Borth. They were not linked.

> **Borth in 1845 – according to the 'Apportionment of rent charges in lieu of tithes'**
> **Upper Borth**: 2 farmhouses, 2 boathouses, 29 cottages, 4 two-storey buildings, a smithy and a Methodist chapel
> **Morfa**: 5 lime kilns, 70 cottages, 9 houses, a church schoolhouse and an inn

The *Pevsner Buildings of Wales* described the village as having an 'insubstantial look, with flimsy cottages edging the main street and the more solid buildings sea-battered and roughly altered'.

A surprising number of people owned their own homes, including 14 cottages owned by women. However, this obviously reflects that many women were left to cope on their own because their husbands never came back from sea. Ownership of houses may well have evolved through the tradition of 'tŷ unnos' (one-night house). A tradition going back to the Middle Ages, it meant that any individual – who could erect a house on common land in one night, with its own roof in place and smoke coming from the chimney by dawn – could then be entitled to own that land. Apparently, in Borth, the first walls would be made of peat blocks but, after a year and a day, the walls would be rebuilt from packed earth or beach stones. It meant, of course, that many of these cottages developed from very simple structures, with walls made of puddle clay reinforced with stone corners, and a roof thatched with bulrushes or made of turf.

Inside there would be a partition between the two rooms.

The upper end was the kitchen with the hearth, and the roof being the ceiling. The lower end was the family bedroom and that had a boarded ceiling. There was a loft between the ceiling and the roof, which could be made into an extra bedroom as the family expanded. As many as ten to twelve people were often cramped into these cottages.

This simple description gives clues as to how villagers earned their living. Obviously, it was a farming community. All over Cardiganshire there were lime kilns which made it possible to enrich the thin soil. A smithy provided for the needs of horse owners.

It was actually the needs of the farming community which began the flurry of maritime activity that climaxed in the late nineteenth century, and from which the men of Borth emerged as prosperous ship captains or owners.

In around 1700 it was realised that spreading burnt lime could enrich soil on the coast of Wales. Lime kilns were built but limestone had to be brought in by sea, along with coal / crushed anthracite to burn it. Gradually, the ships of Cardigan Bay became carriers of the mineral wealth of the area too – copper ore, slate, lead ore, iron and coal. These vessels were small, only capable of carrying 50 to 75 tons of cargo. It was a more productive form of transport, rather than attempting to move things around on the poor roads.

For centuries Borth men had had a connection with the sea, mainly because of the herring shoals which appeared in the autumn. In 1728 the vicar of Llandre was given the tithe of 'herring and other fish from four fishing boates belonging and mooring in Borth and Aberleri'. On 5 October 1745 it was recorded that 47 boats, of about 12 tons each, captured 2,160 maces of herring in one night! Apparently, there are 550 herring in a mace, so the catch came to well over a million, enough to fill 1,000 barrels. Fishing boats also went in search of crustaceans and cockles in the Dyfi estuary.

The Portuguese story

One story from that time is the tale of the Portuguese ship that ran aground on the rocks on 22 November 1746 at Borth. The cargo of the sunken ship helped replenish the cellars and larders of Plas Gogerddan, some five miles away. It was said that members of the crew afterwards were so scared of the tempestuous seas that they settled in the surrounding districts and found ready work in the local lead mines. This may explain the swarthy dark looks of some local inhabitants.

In sworn evidence found in documents at the National Library of Wales, it was said that David James and Edward Williams of Borth, 'did help to secure several puncheon of oyle, lemons, orange, chest, pomegranates, ropes, cork, wood and one saile stranded on ye shore within each lordship of John Pugh Pryse'. These were later carried to the Gogerddan estate by the agent David Morgan and his assistant Richard Hughes. For performing this duty they were given ten pounds and five guineas, respectively.

There's an anecdotal tale of how one Portuguese sailor had the villagers attack him for his boots! The boots were waterlogged and tight, so the villagers had to cut off his legs to get the boots. As the sailor lay dying in pain, he cursed the guilty men of Borth for nine generations.

Other stories surfaced regularly. It was mentioned, in a letter from local mariner A.C. Vaughan to J. Glyn Davies, that an inbound master and an outbound master once had a screaming match after a near miss in Aberystwyth harbour. The Borth man was called a 'Portuguese' by the other captain, something which he resented bitterly after being reminded of the horror that befell the Portuguese sailor and his curse in 1746.

Another variation of this traditional story was that a Portuguese sailor was killed after being chased northwards by the villagers, until eventually caught and murdered near Ynyslas bridge.

This grisly story and other ghost tales of foreign sailors haunting the sand hills of Ynyslas were no doubt used to prevent people from investigating any wrecks further. There were those who were convinced that the lights they saw at night were of supernatural origin, and to be treated carefully. The fact that the story gained such currency, however, does say something about the reputation of Borth sailors. To survive as a master mariner, a man was going to need this gritty determination for self-survival.

The boom years for shipping were the 1850s, partly because of the Crimean War but mainly because at this stage Britain was moving towards its pinnacle of worldwide economic dominance. Larger schooners and brigs of 80 to 120 tons were becoming popular now and these ships were being built within the county.

Then came the last flourish of the great sailing ships before the railways and steamships took over. This was the time when schooners and brigs searched the world for cargo. The *Rowland Evans'* voyages are an indication of how far ships went at this time.

The coming of the railways

The establishment of a railway station at Borth made the village a popular seaside resort. The Aberystwyth and Welsh Coast Railway built the line from Machynlleth to Borth in 1863, and then added the line to Aberystwyth a year later. The two masterminds behind the building of the railway were Thomas Savin and David Davies of Llandinam. It was Savin who saw the potential for middle-class visitors to Borth. He built the impressive row of three-storey Victorian villas, Cambrian Terrace, that led from the station into the village, and also the Cambrian Hotel (which later became known as Pantyfedwen). These buildings, according to a visitor at that time, gave Borth an air of distinction, whereas before it had been described as a 'wretched-looking fishing village'.

I wish I had known the Cambrian Hotel at its finest, when it had Turkish baths, Russian baths, and saline baths! I only knew it when I was a student, when it was a very basic youth hostel. I made beds and washed dishes to gain some pocket money in the holidays. Now, it is completely destroyed.

The summer visitors who came in Victorian times did so on a grand scale. Many would rent houses for an entire month, and bring a nursemaid and cook to take care of the family. The visitors that I remembered in the 1950s, however, came west for the 'industrial fortnight', when the factories of Birmingham closed for their summer break. Most of them stayed at the caravan site on the edge of the village, which had its own shops and entertainment, much to the disapproval of Borth landladies.

The summer visitors in their turn moaned that the pubs were 'dry' on Sundays! At that time the Welsh counties voted individually as to whether pubs would open or close on the Sabbath. Our family used to be very grateful that Borth was 'dry', as our house was only a few doors away from a pub and too frequently, after a Saturday night, we found beer glasses nestling in our front garden!

Three hundred pupils and teachers from Uppingham School in Rutland came to stay in Borth in 1876–7 to avoid an outbreak of typhus in their own part of the world. In doing so they must have restored faith in the health giving qualities of the village. Three hundred bedsteads and mattresses were unloaded on Borth station platform!

The Friendship Inn had opened for business in 1860, with Captain David Hughes in charge, giving his premises the name of his old ship. In 1871 the Railway Hotel opened. By the middle of the next century times had changed – only two of the chapels flourished, but all four pubs did a roaring trade!

Storms

Dramatic photographs on television show us today the sea beating on the shore. This was no new thing in Cardigan Bay, as the storms of the nineteenth century exemplify. An Uppingham schoolmaster recorded: 'A holiday due to the tempestuous weather. The waves, mountain high, were breaking upon the houses of Morfa, so the poor people were in imminent danger. The houses were flooded and the furniture floating about the houses. Never had such an event occurred in the memory of any man living in the village.'

The boys of Uppingham School helped after the storm, repairing defences, rescuing furniture, building stone barricades and restacking peat. The headmaster commented: 'the pleasure of helping other people was common to all and many of the young hearts, which tasted that pleasure in this rough day's labour, will have gained an impulse of prompt helpfulness that may serve them in other and ruder storms than that which shook the frail homes of these friendly villagers.'

Ironically, it was that storm which prompted John Beynon, a local builder, to realise the importance of sea defences. He built a series of saddleback groynes along the beach. It was never easy defeating the sea at its most powerful however, and sometimes they made walking along the beach difficult.

There was another tremendous storm on 8 October 1896, when the wind blew a high tide onto the beach, destroying seven cottages at the southern end and severely damaging a dozen others. Cottages had been built in rows of six or 12, with alleys in between as access and, even more important, as a way of disposing night soil – the village only had 70 privies!

A strange tale my grandmother used to tell me of the 1896 storm was a story about a clergyman. He left his boots outside his door to be polished, only to find the next morning that the sea had carried them to the door of the chapel where he was expected to preach that day!

A storm that I remembered vividly as a child was in the

1950s when we lived at Ardwyn, a house on the sea side of the road. I was waiting in the sitting room for our favourite radio programme to come on. When I popped my head around the door, I found my mother brushing the water gushing in under the back door and down the passageway out to the front door. Apparently, I was not at all alarmed, even when we did eventually sit down and listen to the wireless and a crisp BBC voice announced that 'our selection of poetry tonight would not be complete without a poem about the sea'!

CHAPTER 7

The medicine chest

IN 1954, WHEN I was 11 years old, my grandmother and Aunty Get dragged a medicine chest out of its hiding place. It was the most startling of family treasures. They knew how much I loved old things, especially if they were connected to stories from the past.

'Now you can tell the story of the captain and his last days on his ship, the *Rowland Evans*,' they chorused, expecting me to be excited.

But at first I was disappointed. The medicine chest was nothing very much, I thought. From the outside it was just an ordinary wooden box, but, when I opened it up, I saw a glittering array of glass bottles. They were labelled with long-forgotten medical remedies, some even marked as poison. There was also an alarming hypodermic syringe, which looked as if it could be used on an elephant. There was also a booklet addressed 'To the owners and captains of the Merchant Navy', which contained instructions on how to take care of sailors' common illnesses.

This was the beginning of what sparked my quest to find out the true story of the captain and his ship. Looking back, I'm not sure if it was Aunty Get or my grandmother who told me the actual story of their father's medicine chest. Both loved a good tale, and needed no prompting to talk about family history. Listening to stories was always a part of my childhood.

As a very young child I had spent a great deal of time away from school with painful tonsils. My mother would comfort me with stories she invented about the china ornaments on the shelf above the fireplace in my bedroom – the little sailor by his boat, the Chinese dragons around the soapstone carvings, and the florid blossoms on Edwardian china. Her tales were my introduction to the world of stories, and, as an only child, books became my closest companions. The books which I enjoyed most were historical novels, like the work of Margaret Irwin, Rosemary Sutcliff and Cyntha Harnett. Where films were concerned, my mother smiled when my reaction to the film, *Kind Hearts and Coronets*, was not horror at the number of murders, but glee that everything was 'old fashioned'. Part of me always seemed to love living in the past.

Aunty Get had a passion for telling biblical tales. She hung pictures on the wall, like the *Judgement of Solomon*. But I mostly loved listening to stories of old Borth, and the most exciting was the real-life drama of the sinking of the *Rowland Evans*. I was never told about the captain's disgrace, but there was, nevertheless, enough excitement in what my aunts told me to fascinate me!

I attempted to write the story. I also drew the scene of the wreck, with hats floating in the air, hair blowing in the wind, and terrified faces screaming. I lost the drawing but kept the story I wrote and kept trying to make it more interesting. I tried hard to recreate the drama of the sinking ship, the tension among the crew, and the joyful reunion of the family on their return to Borth to such a fine feast. It made a good tale as an 11 year old, but little did I know it was not the complete truth.

My father's version of the medicine chest story

My father was raised on a smallholding in Montgomeryshire. One of a family of five children, there were very few treasures in his family, so he knew how important it was to preserve both the physical objects and written history of the family. He suggested that the medicine chest be put on display to as many people as possible.

The best-known museum in Wales then was called St Fagans Welsh Folk Museum. It had been founded by Iorwerth Peate in 1946 to record the lives of everyday people. It was based on the Swedish open-air museum Skansen in Stockholm, which displayed houses from the past, furnished from the period in which they were built, and brought from all over the country. St Fagans also included exhibition space for objects that were used in the working life and leisure of farmers and sailors. Museums were moving away from simply recording the lives of the rich. The lives of farmers, sailors and industrial workers were as important as the aristocracy.

My father appreciated the value of the historical objects the Evans sisters owned. He wrote to St Fagans asking them if they would be interested in a large polished oak chest and a ship's medicine chest with its old phials and hypodermic needles.

There follows an extract from my father's letter, written at Ardwyn, Borth, donating the chest to St Fagans Museum, 22 May 1954.

This chest has the most interesting history. It belonged to Captain John Evans, Mrs Lewis' father, of Saxatile, Borth, formerly known as Morfa and one of the two oldest houses in Borth. Captain John Evans used to go to sea in small brigs of about 600 to 700 tons, with a crew of about 9 – himself, 1st, 2nd and 3rd mates, and other crew. He used to trade out of Spain and South America, often spending 3 to 4 years in coastal trading in South American waters. He was his own doctor and prepared for anything!

On returning from his voyages, his wife would travel to meet him to Antwerp, Dunkirk or the French ports. On the last occasion the medicine chest went to sea, Captain Evans was commanding a brig known as the *Rowland Evans* which was built at the shipyard of Derwenlas, Machynlleth, which is now unapproachable, even by a rowing boat. He had returned from a long voyage and his wife had travelled to Antwerp to meet him. As the ship was proceeding down the English Channel off Falmouth and on the way to Cardiff, it encountered a terrible storm. They battled with the ship for two days but it became clear that the ship was about to break up. They were obliged to abandon ship and put to sea in the ship's one lifeboat, the captain and 9 crew, Mrs Evans and the medicine chest and stores. In the lifeboat they proceeded around Land's End, and off Lundy Island they decided to proceed directly to Borth where their arrival on the beach caused a stir. This was about 1885. The worthy captain was soon at sea again, but he and his whole crew were lost at sea in the 1890s.

He also added that the captain had said: 'in the old days there were wooden ships with iron men, but in modern times there are wooden men in iron ships!'

Iorwerth Peate became interested in our humble medicine chest. It was arranged that the museum van came to collect it. I felt very proud. Something of ours was going to be on display at a national institution.

The visit to St Fagans

Strangely enough, I didn't see that chest again until 2010! I got in touch with Ellen Phillips at the museum and she very kindly gave up her Saturday morning to show it to us, as it was no longer on display in the main museum.

The day we visited was a hot July day. We were taken into the coolness of the storeroom. The museum had grown so large that it was now not always possible to display all its objects. Donors can request to see objects kept in storage. In fact, as we walked through the serried ranks of enormous harps and bardic chairs, we realised just how much material has been donated over the years. There is, however, something rather sad about those once treasured belongings rarely being exposed to general view.

As usual, with things we remember from childhood, the sea chest seemed to me to have shrunk in size. Disappointingly, the hypodermic needle that had fascinated me so much as a child was inside a drawer that was now too fragile to open.

The museum, however, had thoughtfully given me a list of the contents of the little glass bottles where it was still possible to read the labels. They had also photocopied the letter my father had written when the sea chest was presented to the museum.

It was not until we left that I opened my father's handwritten letter to the museum. A wave of emotion flooded over me. My father's illness had made him a rather shadowy figure in my childhood as he had died when I was 14 years old.

He had been in and out of hospital most of my childhood. The letter explained how he had taken over looking after Aunty Get's treasured possessions, and that my grandmother had agreed that the sea chest could go to the museum.

At this time Aunty Get's memory was starting to fade. It's not surprising, therefore, how inaccurate her account might have been about what happened to the *Rowland Evans*. After Aunty Get's death, my grandmother began a decline into acute old age that made her so confused that she wandered out into the street in her nightgown and was even known to stand on a desk and beat the windows with her cane, giving the impression that she was being imprisoned. My mother explained that she had been the most wonderful mother to her after her own mother had died. It was then I began to understand the sadness of dementia.

Later I discovered just how confused the dates and places were in my father's letter. The fact that the ship had left Antwerp for Cardiff, sailing past Falmouth, eventually sinking off Lundy Island, was incorrect. It did not sink in 1885 and there is no mention of the captain's disciplinary hearing.

The impression was also given that the same crew were with him when they drowned in the West Indies. My father wasn't aware that John Evans had not sailed as a captain after his disciplinary hearing.

It was fascinating to catch a glimpse of my father's personality in this letter. He obviously had a sense of humour; he described John Evans as the 'worthy' captain. My father had added his own romantic touches to the story, but he had genuinely believed the information given to him by the old ladies. He had not thought about why we still had the sea chest. Surely, it would have been drowned with the captain on his last trip.

Many of the bottles in the sea chest had lost their labels. The museum made a diagram of the position of the bottles in the sea chest. Even a superficial look at the list of contents showed what a strange mixture of folklore remedies and Victorian science formed the basis of my great-grandfather's collection of medicines.

A medicine chest was a vital part of a ship's equipment. An Act of Parliament had decreed this in 1850, stipulating that, 'every ship navigating between the United Kingdom and any place out of the same, shall have and constantly keep on board a sufficient supply of medicines and medicaments suitable to accidents and diseases arising on sea voyages'.

The same act laid down strict rules about providing the crew with lime or lemon juice, sugar and vinegar after they had been consuming salt provisions for ten days. The lack of fresh produce on long journeys must have been very difficult, and the danger of scurvy was constant.

The owner of a merchant ship was also responsible for expenses incurred for injuries, or hurt suffered by any member of crew in the service of the ship. It was not allowed for the expense to be taken out of a crew member's wages. There were penalties for selling bad medicine too.

Medicines concerned with the movement of the sailors'

bowels were very important. Toilet arrangements known as 'bucket and chuck it' could not have helped matters.

Shocking to us these days was the lack of concern about the presence of opium in so much medication. The most notorious of these concoctions was laudanum. This was a mixture of opium, wine and various spices. At that time it was the most common way of cheering up the spirits at the end of a hard day. It was also popular all over Britain among the working classes. It was used for conditions such as rheumatism, sleeplessness, diarrhoea, coughs, colds, and depression. Captain Evans listed it clearly as a poison. Just as well he did, for there seemed to be little effort to give exact measures and dosages. It could so easily kill if administered in the wrong proportions. As a good Nonconformist, he would have been shocked had he known of the intoxicating effects of the drug.

Two pamphlets were given to captains to instruct them in how to treat common illnesses in their crews. The titles on Captain Evans' pamphlets are no longer legible.

Some Borth men seemed to have a natural flair for treating illnesses. John Beynon could set bones and knew all about herbal medicines. William Jones used wool as a healing medium; he would bind certain parts of the body with woollen twine or cloth until the patient was cured.

Captain Evans was not so confident. His impulse was to put the sickest men in hospital when they reached port. It was a heavy responsibility for the captain, as there would be no doctor on board merchant ships. The captain was expected to see to any of his crew who were sick with only the instructions found in pamphlets.

Some attempt was made to keep captains informed about medical knowledge. For the Royal Navy, Sir William Burnett produced a manual. In 1852, T. Spencer Wells published a book called *The Scale of Medicines*, which tried to help captains in the Merchant Navy in the same way. He noted that 'a ship is a floating dwelling' and so needs to be kept scrupulously clean. The Victorians were learning, from the experiences of city slums, just how dangerous dirty, cramped conditions could be.

The importance of cleanliness meant that captains were very careful to clean out the hold after any dirty cargoes. One wonders if the story my grandmother told of ships carrying guano excrement could have been true.

CHAPTER 8

Rattling good yarns

THE STORIES I began to learn about my past had been formed from listening to local rattling good yarns told to me during my childhood. Take for example the story of Rhys Ddwfn's special plant.

Once there was a magical leader called Rhys Ddwfn. Oh, his people were such handsome people. They had blonde hair that gave them a special radiance, delicate skins and amazingly tiny builds. They were fine farmers. Their animals were tended so carefully that they grew strong and supple, and their plants, crops and flowers bloomed gloriously. Surely they must have the most wonderful 'green fingers'?

In fact, they grew one special clump of plant. It was said that if you were to step on it you would be able to see clearly their mystical land in all its loveliness. Step off the clump and you would remember nothing of its enchantment!

Eventually, the crops failed to do as well as usual and the people's bellies rumbled with hunger. They had to learn new skills to replace their farming skills. They could then be found doing such things as quilting, carving dolls and love spoons, forging cast-iron pots, making benches and stools. They traded at Cardigan market.

One of the buyers, Gruffydd ap Einion, began to take a genuine interest in how they organised their lives. He loved to talk and discuss their ideas with them.

They, in turn, took him to their magic plant, and when he stood upon it he amazingly saw before him all the knowledge in the world that had been kept safely in forests and books. It was as though he had found the perfect Utopia. He was heartbroken when he stepped off the plant and the fabulous land disappeared behind a curtain of mist.

Gruffydd stroked his beard thoughtfully and said to Rhys Ddwfn, 'I am impressed that you and your people seem to have no idea of greed for money. I can see that you have no currency.'

'True.'

'And please satisfy my curiosity. Why is there no crime among you?'

Rhys Ddwfn smiled. 'Just as Ireland has been blessed with a soil where no venomous snakes can live, so here in our land no lawbreaker can live.' Rhys picked up a handful of sand and said, 'Look at these grains of sand. They blend together perfectly, so this kind of union exists among my followers. It has happened because I have rid the land of those people who care only for their own personal gain. Our people have been taught to honour their parents and their ancestors, to live with their wives faithfully and to care for their children and elderly. You can see it has made a happy place.'

'I wish our mortal lives were so rich!'

Sailors coming in from the sea caught a glimpse of these magical lands – lovely green islands. Yet, when they tried to land, a curtain of mist and rain blocked it all out. But they knew that somewhere lived very special people.

Today there are people who might want to walk the causeway to Rhys Ddwfn's land. But they can only catch a glimpse of it through the watery haze. But the challenge is still there, reaching out to be touched. Just a few know of the wonders of that good and faithful life, and know it's a real thing and will long to be in that charming place.

The above story of course has no factual historical basis,

but the belief in magic has been there for centuries, especially among the farming community. Clinging on to magic and dreams of a better world can be the only hope in a harsh world.

When I was growing up local tales explained more threatening events, too. The drowning of Cantre'r Gwaelod, the Lowland Hundred, off the coast Cardigan Bay, is one such story deeply engrained in the memory of countless Welsh mariners.

The most popular version of the Cantre'r Gwaelod story centres around a great flood in the sixth century, and this tale went on being told and retold, becoming especially popular in Victorian times.

All versions of the Cantre'r Gwaelod story have a person being blamed for the great flood; they are always guilty of some sinful wickedness, too. Seithenyn was the most frequently accused, and his sin was drunkenness.

The following version comes from the Victorian writer Thomas Love Peacock in his book, *The Misfortunes of Elphin* (1829).

Long, long ago there was no such place as Cardigan Bay, no great coverlet of glittering sea, but instead there was a glorious rich agricultural land of green fields, golden corn and sleek cattle. There was enough land to be divided up into sixteen prosperous townships where many traders visited. Yet, there was always anxiety that the sea would come flooding onto the land. The king, Gwyddno Garanhir, wisely decided to build dykes, wells, drains and sluice gates to protect the land, with guards in watchtowers to ensure that the walls did not cave in. Floods were always a real threat in a land that was below the level of the sea.

The man put in overall charge of this was Prince Seithenyn. He seemed a man of high birth, but he had a fault. He was a drunkard. In fact, courtiers at the time laughed, and it was said, according to gossip, that he was one of the three most famous drunkards in Britain. You could tell so by his purple complexion and unsteady gait, and of course he was not as careful about his duties as he should be.

Luckily, another prince called Teithrin had been given control of the other watchtower further down the dyke, and it was he who realised how neglected the walls had become. He went off to find Seithenyn to tell him exactly how things were.

As usual, he found him feasting and drinking deeply from his golden cup. It was a large cup full of fine wine, so fine a wine that Seithenyn's brain was addled and he took no real notice of what he was being told.

'Drunken sot! I have nothing to do but report him to the mighty king himself, Gwyddno Garanhir,' Teithrin muttered to himself.

He set off immediately for the king's palace, only to find his way blocked by a bristling army officer who told him sharply, 'You have no invitation, and as far as I can see, you are no prince and only princes are allowed in.'

Teithrin looked down at his sweaty, stained tunic and saw that his boots were muddy. He knew that he did not look his rank. If only the king's son Elphin had been there, he would have been able to tell the pompous young guard officer who he was.

'Where is Prince Elphin?'

'Gone fishing.'

Teithrin knew well enough where Elphin would be, so he set off for the fishing banks of the River Mawddach and, sure enough, he found Elphin sitting under an alder tree watching the river swirl and eddy, hoping to catch a plump brown trout in the bountiful river's depths.

All was serene and peaceful and it seemed a perfect spring evening until the clouds darkened and a scream rang out. 'Beware, beware the torment of Gwenhudiw.'

The two men went pale. They knew what it meant, as

Gwenhudiw was thought to be the shepherdess of the deep. Her power was such that she drove her sheep, the white waves, with the power of a terrifying ram into the place of drowning from which men did not return. In fact the king, Gwyddno Garanhir, was so alarmed by her destructiveness that he had moved his palace as far away from the sea as possible.

This had made Elphin nervous enough, but as he listened to Teithrin and his warning about the broken dyke, he decided not to bother his father. The pair of them should see to Seithenyn himself immediately, and return him into some sort of discipline.

Imagine their horror when they found him even drunker than usual.

He greeted them with, 'Welcome, you four.'

'But sir, there are only two of us.'

Then, to their horror, they realised what was the matter. The man was so sozzled, he was seeing double! Even worse, he would not believe any warnings about the state of the dyke.

'The men of old who built those sea defences would not make such mistakes, you fools. Get away from me and let me drink in peace.' Seithenyn pounded the table in anger. Then, for moment, he suddenly became alert as he heard the terrible voice, 'Beware, beware the torment of Gwenhudiw.'

He had no idea who Gwenhudiw was or what her power was.

'Who are you? My enemy?' Seithenyn shook his sword at whatever was cursing him.

Then Elphin told him, 'Your enemy is the sea.'

'The sea!'

As if to answer him, the great mountain of the ninth wave mounted up in front of him, its white foam blew into his face until he could see nothing nor understand anything and all he could do was wave his sword menacingly above his head, crying havoc and destruction to all. Somehow, he managed to stagger drunkenly to his feet and then found himself slithering off the parapet of the watchtower, still waving his sword until he disappeared into the depths of the deep itself.

Teithrin and Elphin stood open-mouthed in horror but they did not move. Elphin said, 'We can do nothing for Seithenyn but we can rescue the women.' Already, Angharad, Seithenyn's daughter, and her maidens had taken down spears from the wall to protect them from the dangers that were to come.

In fact, a worse danger was coming. The fearsome power of those waves would destroy the walls, thereby allowing the sea to destroy all in front of them.

Making their way by moonlight, the sad little procession made their way in terror to the safety of Gwyddno Garanhir's palace. When daylight came, the king took them up to the mountain so they could see what damage had been done.

It was worse than they had imagined. They could not believe it. No green fields were left. It seemed as if every dyke had been destroyed and the whole of the beautiful land of Cantre'r Gwaelod had disappeared below the sea. Was there ever such a tragedy? Its magnitude was enough to last through the many generations who still search for the sunken forest's appearance, and on the night of a spring tide listen and shiver with apprehension, waiting for the bells chiming from the sea defences to warn of the coming terror of a flood.

*

I understood what was at the core of this story and the reason why the legend is so persistent in Ceredigion.

The story I had heard from the three sisters about the sinking of the *Rowland Evans* formed itself from the above kind of tales. The following descriptive piece is typical of what I wrote.

The masts creaked, the sails shook, the wind howled and the crew of the *Rowland Evans* knew enough to know that danger was coming. A terrible storm was gripping the ship.

Down below the men felt the ship go up and down, up and down the mountainous waves.

Poor Sarah Evans, the captain's wife, trembled with fear. She tugged at her husband's sleeve piteously. She rarely sailed with him on his voyages. Other Borth women did sail with their captain husbands but Sarah was delicate. She felt it strongly, the terrible realisation that the ship was in peril.

'Look, there's water coming in.' She could hear it swishing around the decks.

'Man the pumps,' her husband shouted.

The crew did their best but it was doing little good. The water was still rising through the decks. The crew were surprised. The *Rowland Evans* was a big ship. Surely it would survive better than this, but the pumps were doing no good.

The captain understood now what had to be done, especially as the storm showed no sign of abatement. Putting his hands to his mouth, he bellowed, 'Abandon ship. Abandon ship.'

The crew were slow to react. He had to get them into action.

'Hurry up! Do you want to be one with the dead of Cantre'r Gwelod? Come on. Lower the boat. Carefully, carefully, think of Mrs Evans.'

The crew all stared at her. She seemed so fragile, pale faced and rigid with fear. They were rough men, not used to delicate movement but they were careful with Sarah and the boat. Two of the men even had the good sense to put the ship's medicine chest in the boat in case of sickness. After all, they could not be sure what might happen now.

'Where to, captain?' one of the men asked.

'Borth, of course.' The captain did not look at any of them. They probably thought it was a ridiculous choice but he did not care. He just wanted his wife home safe and sound with their children. Through pouring rain, he turned and looked at his sinking ship for the last time and felt a wave of grief for the loss of a vessel that had served him so well.

He was right. The men were surprised by his choice. There were other ports that were nearer, but the captain's navigation skills were sound and surely he must know this part of the world well. He would know that it was one of the safest places to land.

In his mind the captain saw those three miles of golden sand that stretched from the headland of Upper Borth to the Dyfi estuary at Ynyslas. He had it all in his head. He could see them landing by that pile of stones in the centre of the beach that led up to his own house, Saxatile.

Thankfully, the storm began to subside but it seemed such a long way to row. Eventually he saw that pile of stones, and all the captain's neighbours, stumbling and shouting their welcome.

Mary Jones hugged Sarah and said, 'I'll tell the girls that you're safe.'

She ran across the road to get them and then they came – the captain's three daughters Jane, Sal and Getta running to meet their parents', half-laughing, half-crying. Their brother William was not with them. He was at sea beginning his own career on a new ship.

Their mother looked at her girls, and proudly wiped tears of joy from her eyes. The girls huddled around her to keep her warm.

'We've make a splendid dinner for you, tonight.' Jane, Sal and Getta smiled.

Meanwhile, the captain was trying to hide his own emotions and turned his attention to supervising the unloading of a large wooden chest. The men standing on the beach recognised it was the ship's medicine chest. Obviously important, but there was no sign of the ship's papers, nautical instruments or their clothes! What cargo had it been carrying? There must have been in an awful panic!

That night nothing else mattered but the feasting, and a fine feast it was too. Even when they were very old, Jane, Sal and Getta remembered it all so clearly, like a picture from a book of fairy tales. The dining room had never looked better – jugs and plates glittering on the massive Welsh dresser, a magnificent hanging press to store the fine linen, fresh bread in the daudarn, and jellies chilling on a sideboard with a splendid marble top. In the centre of the table was a fine suckling pig taken from their own animals kept in the back garden, and slaughtered especially for the feast.

There would have been singing, but not the raucous songs of taverns but hymns and gentle folk songs to celebrate the safe return of their loved ones. There may have been some elderberry wine to drink. Above all, there would be a grand tale to tell that you could go on telling year after year!

*

Indeed, that version of the story went on being told for years within the family until an important phone call made it clear that there was more to the captain's story than I had ever imagined.

CHAPTER 9

The boy in the next desk

STRANGELY ENOUGH, IT was a connection with my childhood that brought me closer to the real story of the sinking of the *Rowland Evans*. It began with a conversation with Gwenllian Ashley, at that time a curator at Ceredigion Museum. We were talking about the treasures I had taken to my home in Brightlingsea, and how they could best be looked after when my time passed. Suddenly, she mentioned a recent book about Borth written by Terry Davies. I remembered that name!

There was a Terry Davies in my class at the school in Upper Borth. I remembered him as a boy nicknamed Texas, and he'd sat in the next row of desks to me. Could it be him? Despite our proximity in the classroom, I had barely spoken to him then. We both went on to Ardwyn Grammar School, but our lives were very separate there. As a young teenager he had a reputation for mischief, and grew to be a positive giant in stature compared to the other boys.

After I left Borth I heard rumours that Terry had gone to live in Australia. But, after his unhappy schooldays, I expected that he was unlikely to have emigrated to start a professional career there.

I thought I would take a look at his book. I was in for a surprise. When I picked up his book, *Borth: A Seaborn Village* (2004), I saw on the back cover that he was now Dr T.A. Davies. He had a PhD in Humanities and had won residencies as an artist and scholar in Australia and America. I was deeply impressed, and I must admit a little envious of his achievements. It was also curious that he had a fascination for the same myths and legends that had filled my imagination over the years. He actually knew the more obscure tales of Taliesin, and of course Cantref Gwaelod. Even more fascinating were recollections of oral stories told by the old master mariners still alive when he was a boy. What amazingly rich characters they were, and what a picture they painted of their lives at sea.

A bigger shock awaited me when I read Terry's second book, *Borth: A Maritime History* (2009). This was an account of Borth's seafaring families, stories of which Terry had a very detailed knowledge. He disentangled the tribes of Davies, Lloyd, Evans, Jones, Hughes and Jenkins etc. Practically every seagoing family in Borth was cited, so I naturally expected Captain John Evans to be mentioned. And, I found him mentioned in the section on women. Why?

Terry began the section about the captain with: 'What may one ask, did Captain John Evans' wife, Jane, think of events in 1882 – in fact, was she complicit in them?' I knew by now the significance of 1882. It was the year of the sinking of the *Rowland Evans*. I knew that his wife had been with him on that voyage, but what guilty secret did Terry think they were hiding.

As I read on, I learned that there had been a disciplinary inquiry after the sinking of the ship. She had been leaking pumps on her journey from Antwerp to Bardsey Island, and the captain thought she would sink. The captain had drilled two holes in the *Rowland Evans* to prevent her sinking in the way of other ships. He gave orders for the ship to be abandoned, put his wife and crew in the long boat, and they headed south until they disembarked – to the crew's amazement – at the captain's front door in Borth!

Terry went on to say: 'The court of inquiry remarked that it was the clearest example of premature abandonment that had ever come to the court's notice. Suffice to say, the captain's certificate was suspended for twelve months and the mate was also censured. With no insurance pay out, perhaps John Evans' intended payout had to be postponed.'

So that romantic story of the welcome home feast for the mariners saved from sinking was tarnished by the suggestion that the scuppering of the ship had some sort of ulterior motive. Perhaps an attempt to win a generous insurance claim?

What exactly was this court of inquiry? Was some sort of criminal activity involved? Had the captain deserved to lose his master's certificate? Why had no one in the family ever hinted at this?

I knew that I had to contact Terry Davies for myself. He'd got the captain's wife's name wrong as she wasn't called Jane, but Sarah. Maybe there were other facts that weren't quite right. Sarah had very lady-like tastes, but had this driven her to nag him into scuppering the ship in order to claim insurance?

Eventually, I plucked up courage to contact Terry. So began a whole series of lengthy Skype calls to Australia, then emails, and then at last we met up in Borth. It turned out to be a delight for both of us to have a conversation after all these years, and to see what kind of adults we had developed into. He was a gentle giant, complete with grandchildren, and both of us were taken aback to find out that we had developed a passionate enthusiasm for research abour old Borth and its inhabitants.

Terry introduced me to the website www.welshmariners. org.uk, which gives the dates of Welsh sea captains and their ships. He sent me copies of lectures by well-known maritime historian, David Jenkins. In return, I was able to give information to the website he was creating himself.

Even after completing two books, Terry was still receiving vast amounts of information about Borth. So he and his wife Amanda set up the website www.maritimehistory.com, which uploaded donated photographs and memorabilia about Borth's maritime history. They added a full portrait of Captain John Evans and I donated that rather severe photograph of the captain and his wife Sarah, a picture of the medicine chest from the *Rowland Evans*, photographs of the ship paintings we owned – the *Sarah* and the *Sarah and Mary* – and information about his son William and his steam-driven ships.

Terry managed to sort out the various John Evanses I included in our family tree. As already noted it was mariner Morgan John Evans who was the founder of the family fortunes. His son possibly sailed the sloop *Mermaid*, and commanded the *Laura and Elizabeth* in 1839.

The website also gives details about the welcome home party for the survivors of the sinking of the *Rowland Evans*, and about the decisions of the Board of Trade inquiry. Terry made the important point that it was a valuable ship, so inevitably there needed to be an examination of its sinking. It was strange that the log, instruments, charts and clothes were left behind on the ship, and that the ship had circled around for so long before sinking. The evidence from the crew about the sinking had been very hostile. Part of the reason why the crew was so belligerent to the captain, Terry felt, was because he had a strict no grog (alcohol) policy aboard ship.

I was now beginning to realise how complicated researching the ship's story was going to be. The first thing to do was to find out about the ship's initial construction. Part of me wanted to prove that I could unearth some new research. I had done a history degree at UCW, Aberystwyth, and I did want to know the truth. I really did not want Captain John Evans to be a villain!

PART III

The Captain's Ship, the *Rowland Evans*

CHAPTER 10

Building the *Rowland Evans*

THE COASTLINE OF Cardigan Bay emerges and submerges and, in the process, radically alters itself. As my father said in his letter to the museum, in our time Derwenlas has ceased to be a port and the village become landlocked, mainly as the result of the building of the railway which pushed the River Dyfi further away from the village.

In the early nineteenth century, however, the River Dyfi was navigable within two miles of the village. Derwenlas was a busy port for goods going to and from Machynlleth. In the shipping boom of the 1850s, it was in a good position to become a boatyard.

During the early days of Derwenlas as a port, it was possible to export oak timber, oak poles for collieries, lead ore and slate. Derwenlas port imported rye, wheat, coal, culm, limestone, groceries and other shop goods. Three boat-building yards developed, and 36 up-to-75-ton wooden vessels made from local oak were built there, mainly to sail around Britain. It was there that our Captain John Evans went searching for a new ship after his first ship, *Sarah*, was lost at sea.

Captain John Evans had worked very hard to find the finances to build as large a ship as a brig. Helped by the 1786 Shipping Act, it encouraged small ship owners to share the ownership of ships by dividing the overall cost into 64 shares, made available to a maximum of 32 people. Captain Evans made very good use of this and was lucky to have the support of yet another John Evans, the owner of a local shipyard.

It must have been exciting to watch your ship being built, for it was quite an undertaking. Amazingly, in the early stages, there would have been no paper plan, but it would have been possible to examine a half-hull model which would show how the ship would look. Then, with a rich supply of seasoned, pliable pine from Labrador, Canada, for the bulkheads, and the splendid strength of Welsh oak trees for the ribs, the ship would then take shape.

There would be a saw pit in which to cut the timber by hand into the required lengths and thicknesses of frames and planks. A box, two feet square and as long as the ship, was attached to a boiler for generating the steam to make the timber in the stove springy and pliable, and to eliminate the risk of fracture. The lid of the stove was daubed in clay to make it airtight. Carpenters unstuck the lid, and put the hot steaming planks into the body of the ship on stocks.

The *Rowland Evans* was one of the last ships to be built on shipbuilding sites at Derwenlas. She floated downriver as a hull on the highest tide. She was then fitted out by riggers who erected the sails, painters and carpenters, rope makers and metalworkers, who would all add the finishing touches to ships.

The real genius behind the building of these ships was Jac y Traeth (John Jones the Beach), who got his nickname from his native parish of Llanfihangel-y-Traethau. He built the largest number of vessels in the area, over 29 keels between 1849 and 1870. Captain Evans would have known Jones well, for he built two of Captain Evans' ships – the schooner *Sarah* in 1852 at Aberdyfi, and the brig *Rowland Evans* in Derwenlas in 1864. It was important that ships could carry heavy cargoes without needing continual repairs. The brig, especially, was intended for long voyages, and was an important step forward in expanding future maritime ventures.

Jac y Traeth complained about how fussy Borth men were. In a drunken fit he was alleged to have said, 'Bury me in the new St Peter's graveyard at Aberdyfi, so that I may have deliverance from these damned Borth men.' Captain John Evans might have been one of those damned men, but he, however, might have had his reasons to complain, for Jac y Traeth frequently exasperated ship owners by the number of projects he had under development at one time. He built ships in Aberdyfi, Penhelig and Ynyslas, as well as at Derwenlas. Yet Jac took his shipbuilding very seriously, and there was a tale of him knocking down the corner of a house – which involved moving a sick old lady from her bed – so that a ship he was building could be pulled across the road and down to the water!

There were always those, however, who would defend the independence of Borth men. For centuries the villagers had survived on nothing but the seasonal shoals of herring and the gathering of peat. It was maintained that such poverty had made Borth men brave, pious, resourceful and thrifty.

The man who started shipbuilding at Derwenlas, and in the process gave employment to many Borth men, was Rowland Evans. He was a strong supporter of Independent churches. Captain John Evans would have admired him for that. This shipyard owner came from Dinas Mawddwy, where he was originally a farmer and bark merchant in an area rich in trees. He eventually became more ambitious, and buying wood became his business. In the 1850s he started to arrange for wood to be used in the building of ships, including in 1852 the 76-ton schooner, the *Sarah and Mary*.

Eventually, the trading ports were closed down when the new railway line cut through the main river dock and the river was diverted by the new embankment.

On 21 November 1856, according to *The Caernarvon and Denbigh Herald*, Rowland Evans died a strange death in Aberystwyth:

A very melancholy accident occurred in this place on Monday night last. On the morning of Tuesday, a body very much bruised was discovered at the foot of the Rock on the north side. It was immediately conveyed to a house in the church yard and was with great difficulty recognised to be Mr. Rowland Evans of Morben near Machynlleth, farmer and extensive timber and bark merchant, aged 65. The last period to which he can be traced was nine o'clock on Monday night, about which time he is supposed to have taken a walk in the direction of the castle grounds, and the night being dark, to have slipped over a precipice in going towards a seat a few yards further on. Traces of the ground being disturbed were visible, and the situation of the body, no doubt, could be entertained that he had fallen over. An inquest was held on Wednesday before J.M. Davies, Esquire, and a verdict of 'accidental death' returned. The deceased has left many children to lament his melancholy and untimely death, and was one of the most respected and influential persons in his neighbourhood.

Nobody seemed to think that there was anything sinister about his death, although nine o'clock on a dark November night in Aberystwyth seemed a strange time for a walk. The disturbed ground could have been the result of a severe fall after an epileptic fit.

His son, John Evans of Morben Isaf, thought it appropriate to name the first of the brigs to be built in the shipyard after his father. He was only 23 when his father died, but he was quickly involved in building three schooners and a smack, and the selling of bark to Machynlleth tanneries, and timber to other shipbuilders in the area. He was obviously a skilful businessman for, of the four new ships, he was either the majority shareholder or the outright owner, not to mention the fact that he had inherited shares in ships his father had built before he died.

Then he moved into building two brigs, the largest ships ever built on the Dyfi.

Brigs

Brigs were impressive undertakings, for they had two square-rigged masts. They were larger than a schooner and tended to vary in length.

Brigs were popular as a standard cargo ship. Seen as 'fast and well sailing', they required a relatively large crew to handle the rigging. A brig was not easy to sail into the wind, but a skilled brig captain could manoeuvre it with ease and elegance.

A brig could, for instance, turn around almost on the spot. They were vessels which foundered if they had been insufficiently reinforced, say to carry slate, or if they went on being sailed year after year, after year. No ship loaded to her scuppers with a dead cargo could stand up in a severe gale. It could make a man nervous. An old Welsh mariner was heard reflecting on being aboard one: 'I would not sail her if she were bound for heaven with a cargo of Bibles.'

The launching of the *Rowland Evans*

The *Rowland Evans* was launched in great style. This is how it was reported in the *North Wales Chronicle*, 8 April 1865:

Morben near Machynlleth – launch

On Tuesday last a fine brig was launched from the building yard of Mr John Evans, Morben Wharf. This fine vessel is classed A1 at Lloyds for twelve years, and is to be commanded by Captain John Evans, late master of the *Sarah* of Aberdovey. She is well built and reflects no small degree of credit on Mr John Jones of Aberdovey, the master builder. The cheers of the crowd who witnessed the ceremony were deafening as she glided slowly, yet majestically, into her proper element. After the launch the hospitable owner, Mr John Evans, entertained a host of friends at Morben Hall, where every success was drunk to the new vessel in sparkling champagne.

A wide range of shareholders were involved, as much more money was needed to build a brig. It was going to be a change in the way Captain John Evans sailed, for now he could sail large distances, but wisely he initially clung to warm waters. Hanging on to ships' rigging in ice-cold waters in the northern oceans must have been horrendous. He still needed strong young men to handle that rigging, and increasingly he turned to youthful foreigners. Cardiganshire men were usually the mates, and he often trained up members of his family, like his son William and his nephew Thomas Pryse. Yet, it is noticeable that crews were no longer so tightly bound by family and local connections as they had been on the smaller ships. Best to have foreigners aboard, who knew the currents and the local winds.

CHAPTER 11

The ship's destinations

LARGER SHIPS COULD no longer set out from ports near their captains' homes. They were now part of a bigger pattern of Welsh maritime ventures. Voyages began from Swansea, Cardiff, Newport, Liverpool and London or even Antwerp. It's been difficult to work out exactly how much time the captain spent with his family in Borth between each voyage. Wife Sarah was left alone to bring up her family for much of her life. She rarely chose to go to sea with him. Their daughters also had no taste for life on the ocean wave.

The Voyages of the *Rowland Evans*
1865: Liverpool – Rio de Janeiro – New York – Falmouth
1866: Swansea – Lisbon – Bristol
1867: Cardiff – Barbados – Bristol
1867–8: Cardiff – Constantinople – ports along the Rhine – Sea of Azov – Dublin
1868: Cardiff – Berbice – London
1869: Cardiff – Palma, Majorca – Antwerp
1869: Antwerp – Galatz – Palermo – Falmouth – Rotterdam
1870: Rotterdam – Montevideo – Buenos Aires – Bristol
1871: Newport – Buenos Aires – Rosario – Liverpool
1871–2: Liverpool – Buenos Aires – Paysandú – Antwerp
1873–4: Antwerp – Rio de Janeiro – Rosario – Concepción – Liverpool
1873: Liverpool – Buenos Aires – Liverpool

1875: South Shields – Stettin – Sundsvall – Cádiz – Paysandú
1876: South Shields – Lisbon – Cádiz – Montevideo
1877 Cardiff – Buenos Aires – Liverpool
1878: Liverpool – Rosario – Buenos Aires – Plymouth
1879: Cardiff – Buenos Aires – Paysandú – Bristol
1880: Cardiff – Rio Grande – Buenos Aires – Rio – Montevideo
   – Aberystwyth
12 December 1882: Antwerp to Bardsey Island, where it sank

His voyages took him to ports which were expanding in the second half of the nineteenth century. The captain had good navigational skills and business acumen. He never moved to his next destination without a new cargo. That was not just for commercial reasons but for safety reasons too, for a brig, as noted, would need heavy ballast. If it was empty of cargo, it could topple over.

There are few records of what goods were carried on the *Rowland Evans*. More than likely, these would have been staples in a booming industrial economy, such as coal, timber, leather hides, ores, grain, nitrates and raw materials for factories. The ports trading such goods would have had good rail connections or a broad river to move heavy goods inland. Ports such as Liverpool, Antwerp, Rosario, Buenos Aires and South Shields.

Some places were especially difficult to navigate at. Berbice, Guyana, was never popular, for the place was riddled with disease. Few ships left there without some of the men becoming sick. The *Rowland Evans* did a few European trips; the most exotic of which was a trip to Constantinople, with visits to the Danube, the Black Sea, the Sea of Azov and finishing in Dublin. South America was also a favourite destination. By 1880 the ports of Rio de Janeiro in Brazil, Montevideo in Uruguay, and Rosario in Argentina had built splendid railway connections, and their wealth was reflected in their newly-built elegant city centres, with theatres and neo-classical buildings. The *Rowland Evans* avoided the southern tip of the Americas.

There were plenty of Borth men who could tell of the horrors of the fierce storms and high waves around Cape Horn.

South American cities had volatile populations, mainly because slavery was only just coming to an end and vast numbers of European immigrants were arriving, Yet, they must have been vibrant communities selling exports like sugar, cotton, coffee, leather and skins. Captain Evans must have found it difficult to keep discipline among his young crews when he got to port, but they probably rarely ventured away from the quayside taverns, for that was only what they knew.

The stranger choices of places to stop off seemed to be South Shields and Stettin for coal. As a Welshman, ought he not to have been supporting Welsh mines? These ports must have offered coal at a good price. That would have appealed to a 'Cardi', for Cardiganshire folk have a reputation of being tight with money!

I have actually visited Stettin myself, as it was a stop on a Baltic Sea cruise. It felt very curious to be standing on the deck watching the ship enter port. You can imagine the thoughts I entertained. How did it feel to steer so splendid a ship as the *Rowland Evans* into this port? Even today, entering that port is a considerable challenge, and a sailing ship would have needed to be very careful indeed.

During the captain's time, Stettin was in Germany. Being on the River Oder, very large vessels could make their way far upriver. Cargoes exported from there were sugar, corn, lumber, cement and spirits. Cargoes imported were coal, iron ore, paving stones, French wine and herrings. Stettin was also known for shipbuilding. Today, the same cargoes are loaded on the riverbank, but the port is now called Szczecin and is in Poland.

John Evans loved sailing ships passionately, and was never afraid to venture to new ports. The list of places the ship visited seems incredibly numerous and exciting. He knew the

My mother sitting on top of a sandcastle, held tightly by my grandfather.

A happy day on the beach when I was four years old.

Sitting proud in my grammar school uniform, although the tie was never tidy!

My mother's drawing of my father.

Mary Evans of Cwmcethin, the mother of the 'worthy captain'.

© National Library of Wales

Aunty Jane (right) with a friend in the garden.

Sarah Mary as a married lady.

W.T. Lewis' first marriage, in 1901, to Anne Mary Farquar Evans.

Sarah Vivienne Gwynora as a four-year-old child.

Aunty Get with her pupils – she is standing nearest the children on the left.

Aunty Get (front row, right) with her colleagues.

Young Ivor in his boat.

Rex's postcard to Madge, showing his steamship, the *Raithmoor*.

Uncle William's beautiful first wife.

Uncle William in uniform.

Grandma, Aunty Jane and Aunty Get, the daughters of Captain Evans, in extreme old age.

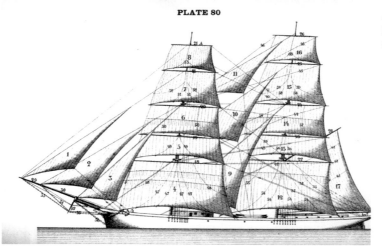

PLATE 80

An illustration of a brig.

The busy port of Stettin in the nineteenth century.

Modern-day Szczecin (Stettin), now in Poland.

Postcard from Antwerp, 1912, showing the Brabo Fountain.

A lace shop in modern-day Antwerp that Sarah would have loved.

Nineteenth-century Antwerp.

Cargo waiting to be loaded in the 1880s.

Handcarts were everywhere in Antwerp.

Peter points to where the *Rowland Evans'* long boat may have landed on Borth beach.

THE fine A 1 Brig ROWLAND EVANS, 209 tons register, 360 deadweight; built at Aberdovey in 1865, and classed A 1 for 12 years; was continued in 1877 for 9 years at a cost of about £1,400; new f.y.m. and overhaul in 1881, cost £400. Dimensions:—101.3 × 25.0 × 13.2. Now lying at Antwerp.

B. BARRY WAKE, 5, Fowkes-buildings, Great Tower-street, London. E.C.

An advert selling the *Rowland Evans.*

An example of Margaret Jones' Berlin work.

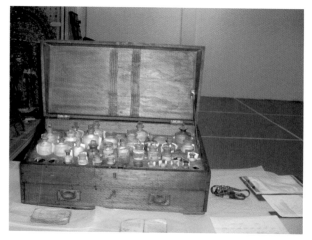

Two views of the medicine chest rescued from the *Rowland Evans*.

The silver cigarette case Uncle William rescued from the streets of St Petersburg during the Russian Revolution.

The *Sarah and Mary* ship owned by the family.

Captain John Evans' first ship, a schooner called the *Sarah*, and named after his wife.

A sail schooner carved as a love token.

An engraved wine glass owned by the Lloyd family who married into the Evans family.

The cliffs at Borth in 2010.

A sweeping view of Cardigan Bay.

A more recent ship in Borth – a crab boat!

Borth railway station platform, the starting point of journeys to London.

London House, with its scars of different lives as a shop, the Welsh Kitchen, and a tandoori restaurant.

Saxatile in 2010.

My mother's pastel of an idealised Saxatile.

A portrait of my mother painted by Barbara Hayes.

Ardwyn in 2010.

Cwmcethin, the childhood home of Captain John Evans.

My old chapel, now converted into a restaurant and cinema.

commercial potential of new trades opening up, yet the risks were clear, and, what must have driven him on was a real strength of character.

CHAPTER 12

The ship's register

ALTHOUGH I NOW live far away from Borth, I still see sailings ships and boats every day of my life as I walk along the River Colne in Brightlingsea. Maybe the smacks and barges that float up and down the River Colne today are mainly the pleasure boats of weekend sailors, but there is always someone who knows their rich maritime history.

John Collins, an archivist from the Nottage Institute, told me about ships' registers. A ship's register gave a description of the ship, its owners and master. Ships' registers began in 1786 when the owners of any British ship with a deck, and of more than 15 tons burden, had to register it with customs officers at its home port. This was followed by a later act in 1852, which laid down that the ownership of any vessel, as already noted, had to be divided into 64 shares. I needed this information to understand the financial affairs of the *Rowland Evans*.

It was a problem finding out where a ship was registered. Where and when a ship was built was found in Lloyd's Register. The next stage was to track down the archives in the area where the ship was built. Easy for the *Rowland Evans*, as it had to be Aberystwyth and the Ceredigion Archives, 'the search room by the sea'. On that day that I visited Ceredigion Archives in 2010, it had a Dickensian feel, with piles of books and papers everywhere. And some of the most sinister scenes for the television programme *Hinterland* were later filmed there.

The ship's register for the *Rowland Evans* arrived on a trolley and was placed on a cushion for ease of handling. Most of the copperplate writing was still very legible. Suddenly, we were back in the world where investing in a ship was a big adventure. The 64 shares of the *Rowland Evans* were owned by a wide range of people, including a farmer, a widow, a merchant, a grocer, a draper, an ironmonger, an engineer, a minister of the gospel and even some merchants from Cardiff, ship chandlers called Willam Peake and his son Luke. Obviously, for some investors there was a practical use, for the ship might carry cargo which was part of their trade, but for many it was the excitement of a secret gamble. Investing in ships had always had a curious allure.

There was a tradition of consortia of farmers, merchants and seaman being involved in the shipping trade, some of whom had got together to actually own small smacks and sloops in the 1840s and 1850s when they were directly concerned with the goods going up and down the coast of Wales. The liability of shareholders holding 60 / 40 shares was unlimited, and each year they took a cut of the profit made by the vessel that was in proportion to their shareholding. Once ships started to travel further afield, shareholdres dreamt of wealth or the charm of foreign ports.

In the first year of its existence, the ship's official owner was John Evans of Morben, and he took eight shares in the ship. The master, John Evans of Borth, took 12 shares. He'd secured £250 at six per cent as a mortgage from London broker Hugh Edwards.

The well-known maritime historian David Jenkins said, in his paper on Derwenlas: 'the more widely spread nature of the shareholding in the *Rowland Evans* perhaps reflects the increased cost of building a vessel twice as large as any previously built at Derwenlas.' It was also interesting that two

Cardiff ship chandlers held shares, which may have been an indication that the yard was building up contacts with ports involved in the deep sea trade. Cardiff's foreign coal exports at this time stood at about 2,250,000 tons per annum.

Then, on 17 October 1868, John Evans of Morben died at the age of 35. The *Aberystwyth Observer* reported the death:

> A fatal accident occurred near Machynlleth on Thursday night. Mr John Evans of Morben, near Machynlleth, when riding home between seven and eight o'clock, was thrown from his horse, which had been startled by an approaching train. The unfortunate gentlemen fell on his head and became insensible, a state from which he never rallied and expired at five o'clock. The deceased was generally respected and his death will be regarded as a great loss to the neighbourhood in which he resided.

It seems rather ironic that his death was due to an incident with a train, for it was the coming of railways that was eventually to change shipping in the area. It also was strange that two men from the same family could die from a blow to the head after a fall. A family history of epilepsy was beginning to look increasingly likely.

Captain John Evans of Borth then became the official owner and bought a further two shares from his widow, Mary Evans. She was not slow to find another husband. Mary Evans, at 41 years old, was a comely lady and soon married Dr Robert Pugh on 3 November 1869. Dr Pugh had acted as coroner into John Evans, Morben's death. Her shipping shares were also purchased by her husband-to-be, and the Aberystwyth ship owner, Richard Delahoyde. Sadly, it was the end of an era, as Morben Isaf ceased being a centre for shipbuilding without John Evans' energetic leadership.

Captain Evans, meanwhile, was steadily increasing his shares. By 1873 he had increased his shares to 18. By 1877 his shares had increased to 36. In October 1877 affairs became complicated. Morgan Owens of Aberystwyth became the official owner of the *Rowland Evans*. Captain Evans had taken out a mortgage from Mr Owens for £350 at six per cent in order to cover his 36 shares, and he still had a £250 mortgage from Edwards to cover his initial 12 shares. In 1881 Morgan Owens sold four of his 36 shares to his daughter.

Something did not seem quite right in the affairs of the master of the *Rowland Evans*. These statistics were later to become important in judgements about the captain's character, as he had taken out a substantial insurance policy with the Aberystwyth and Aberaeron Insurance Club.

As I left Ceredigion Archives, I looked out to sea and saw the faintest sight of Bardsey Island shimmering on the horizon. It was a reminder that, running through the final pages about *Rowland Evans*, of a note that sadly said: 'This Vessel Foundered in Cardigan Bay on the 12 September 1882, Bardsey Island, bearing S.W. by W., distance about 18 miles. Certificate of Registry lost with the vessel. Register closed 25 October 1882.' Yet again, a new revelation of where the ship had sank.

CHAPTER 13

A life on the ocean wave

WHAT WAS LIFE aboard the *Rowland Evans* like? It's possible to build a picture from piecing together contemporary descriptions from novels and memoirs, old photographs and scraps of conversation. I wish the worthy captain had written more letters.

One thing was clear – the life which crews committed themselves to was full of danger. The most terrifying thing would have been climbing the rigging to set, furl and unfurl the sails to suit the weather conditions, especially the top sails.

The bigger ships would have had a specialist sail maker, but on the *Rowland Evans* everyone had to help when sails needed replacing or repairing, also with splicing rope and tarring rigging. The work was precarious, especially as the top of the mast could be as high as 150 feet from the deck. Considerable strength and a steady nerve were needed to furl a heavy sodden sail. Young sailors were told, 'one hand for the ship and one hand for yourself' when climbing rigging.

There were so many other perils to face also. The weather was the most obvious danger, with little warning of advancing storms. In narrow crowded estuaries where ships were often moored, there were also plenty of collisions. There was always the liability of navigational errors leaving ships foundering. One of the most terrifying experiences was a fire aboard, which was often caused by dangerous cargoes igniting. Underlying the loss of men was the fact that few could swim. To give you an idea of how dangerous life at sea was then, between 1879 and 1899, 1,153 ships in British waters went missing and 11,000 lives were lost.

Even if they managed to survive danger, it was never a comfortable life. Personal hygiene could be difficult. Each man had half a bucket of water a day to wash and brew tea. And they were a generation who were brought up to believe that 'cleanliness was next to godliness'. Too many illnesses were caused by dirty conditions. Men's clothes and their bodies therefore had to be clean. There was faith in wearing flannel next to the skin, as it was a way of absorbing perspiration. Most sailors brought two trousers made of moleskin, which when they got wet stood up on their own account and chaffed skin off legs. They also wore dreadfully heavy oilskins in bad weather but, if they fell overboard, this would drag them down to the ocean's depth. This may explain why many men did not learn to swim. Some maintained swimming in a heavy oilskin jackets would be totally impossible anyway.

Crew accommodation was below the fo'c'sle. It was a damp and musty place and dimly lit, often awash with the accumulated debris of smashed crockery and fittings which came adrift in heavy weather. The deck was frequently awash when the vessel was laden with cargo. As David Jenkins says, 'at best a sailor was almost continuously wet and at worse he might be washed overboard with no chance of rescue.' Only the captain and maybe his family had a cabin of their own with a little more comfort.

It was difficult to dry clothes or bedding, but on the South American runs the mattresses could be laid out on the deck in the hot sun to dry. Hammocks and bedding needed to be kept as dry as possible. Sloshing water about when scrubbing the decks was to be avoided, and a technique of cleaning the decks by 'holystoning' was the best way to keep men from rheumatism and catarrh. Rheumatism was a genuine problem and could stop a man working. One young German sailor had to be left behind on a 1871 voyage on the *Rowland Evans* because of his rheumatism.

Bilge water was pumped out every day. Keeping the vessel 'shipshape' was hard work. Holystoning the deck with blocks of sandstone kept it in good order. The decks too needed protection; oakum would be driven into the gaps between planks and covered with tar. In great heat the planks could dry out and contract, so they would need caulking. By this time captains had developed great faith in chloride of zinc, which apparently preserved timber from dry rot, preserved canvas from mildew and fire, eliminated the worst smells and also the possibility of contagious diseases.

Steering and handling the ship in every kind of weather and every strength of wind was mainly the master's responsibility. His most valuable instrument was the compass. Weighing anchor and manning the capstan was done by the whole crew, for it took strength to raise the anchor. Photographs exist of whole crews up on the spar, reefing the topmost sails.

Loading and unloading the ship provoked the most aggravation among crews. This caused more desertions than anything else. Sailing ships were not fitted with derricks and the ship's rigging got in the way of cargo being grabbed by a crane, so tackle would be rigged to the lower yard over each hatchway and tailed down. This was work for the entire crew, and they were expected to unload 100 tons of cargo each working day. Unloading coal in the heat of a South American port must have been unbearable. Often the coal was in sacks, and men walked up one gangway, picked up the sacks of coal, walked down another gangway and unloaded the coal into carts pulled by horses. Wool was shipped in bales, and grain in sacks. Cargo nets hanging from the yard arm were also used. It was back-breaking work whether it was done by the crew or sometimes the port dockers where they had landed.

We have little record of what men did to relax. Captain Evans' hymn singing and Bible readings would be on offer in the cabin of an evening but, as his crews were multinational, they would have found craft activities more to their taste. Wood carving was popular, especially the carving of sail smoothers, which could become quite elaborate considering their original practical purpose was to keep the seams between sails fitting together neatly. Certainly, a good rousing sea shanty would have helped with morale whilst pulling ropes, but there seems little mention on Welsh ships of dancing the hornpipe.

Sailors were paid better than farm labourers, but their money vanished quickly when they got on shore. John Everett, a marine artist, who made several voyages on a square rigged ship, gives an insight in his journal about the sort of men John Evans had to control.

> They were like children. For months together they wanted no money. If you paid them £3 a month or £20 a month, it made no difference to them. No matter what they were paid off with, they got rid of it, or it was stolen from them. In fact, the man who got rid of his pay the quickest boasted about it and was a hero in the fo'c'sle. They had no possessions. Their only ambition was to get drunk and have a woman. They could buy the few things they wanted from the Old Man – he usually had a slop chest. And in a sense, they didn't have to pay for it. It was deducted from their pay at the end of the month, but no money passed hands. And if you were gloriously drunk and didn't remember anything you did for the next few days ashore, it didn't matter.

Such a strange picture we get of life aboard ship! Here were men who were capable of tremendous courage, yet who could also be so incredibly silly. I am not wholly convinced that Borth men were quite so foolish. It's difficult to understand their world from the distance of time, with few personal letters and accounts. However, I suspect that men with wives and families at home would have been a little more careful. Though, I found it was possible to get a picture of discipline aboard the *Rowland Evans*. Captain John Evans might have had 'fatherly' control over a crew who were young and found themselves far from home in foreign parts, but he also got into rages over drunken bouts and foul language.

CHAPTER 14

Crews of the *Rowland Evans*

WHAT SORT OF men did the 'worthy captain' employ as his crew. Photographs of Borth sailors gave the impression of short, rugged men with odd-shaped beards, exuding airs of independence.

As master, John Evans first sailed the schooner *Sarah*, named after his wife. For this ship he would have chosen men from his village. He would have needed only a tiny crew, for the vessel did not travel far. Borth captains had a network of family, friends and acquaintances from other local ports, so there was never any trouble finding crew. However, getting a crew for the *Rowland Evans* was more challenging.

After the loss of the *Sarah* in a Bay of Biscay storm in 1864, his world changed for many reasons. Steamships were beginning to take the most experienced men. His new ship, a brig, would need a far larger crew as it was bound for longer voyages. Men with a wider knowledge of the world and faraway ports would be invaluable. They needed to be physically strong to cope with the rigging, so the emphasis was on muscular, young men.

John Evans must have had to resort to wandering the quaysides of foreign ports to find crews to recruit, or even wander the back streets of ports where the pubs, bars and dance halls attracted sailors on shore leave. He might even have had to resort to a 'crimping establishment'. These were places where sailors would have a drink too many, find themselves overcome with drugs, and wake up the next morning out at sea as the crew member of a strange ship, having been sold by the 'crimper', who ran the bar, to a captain desperate for new crew.

What sort of men were recruited for the *Rowland Evans*? Would it be possible to find out after this length of time? My best source of information was likely to be the National Library of Wales. I had the good fortune to have the assistance of librarian William Troughton there, who with his knowledge of maritime history helped me find my way speedily around the computer catalogues. The most important information came from the 'crew lists' and 'log books' of the *Rowland Evans*.

Crew lists are an absolute godsend to any maritime historian. They were legal documents of agreement between the master and his crew. There were two kinds of documents: one for longer journeys in 'deep sea', where the crew committed themselves for about two years; and crew lists for shorter journeys, not expected to last longer than six months. In Captain Evans' case the longer trips were mainly to South America and the Caribbean, and the shorter trips to Europe and the Mediterranean. Trips to the Caribbean could last for up to twelve months.

The beginning and end of each voyage were clearly marked, but stopping places along the route were more difficult to follow. There was little rest between one voyage and the next. It was usually about one month and, during that time, a ship would have to be unloaded and then loaded again.

These ships appear very small compared with modern-day ships. The explanation, according to David Jenkins:

> In all but the largest ports, the facilities were generally
> primitive. Narrow and shallow approaches that were unsuited
> to big vessels were all too typical and this was particularly
> true of small ports around the coast of Wales. The amount
> of cargo available for any one time was often small, and was

laboriously hand worked; the larger the ship, therefore, the longer the loading time, and protracted periods in port have never been conducive to a ship's profitability in any age.

It was exciting to read the handwriting of men on the crew lists. A few, of course, could only manage a cross by their name, but not many. Most could sign their name with a flourish. It was a thrill seeing John Evans' very own signature.

The crew lists supplied information about what the men had to eat. On the very first page, the master would have to show what food he would supply for each sailor daily. Potatoes and vegetables were not mentioned, as they would only be available for the first few weeks at sea. The basic food was bread, salted beef, salted pork, flour, peas, rice, tea, coffee, sugar and water. Board of Trade regulations laid down that the food supplied should be 'sufficient without waste'. In fact, John Evans gave the exact quantities of the food being carried aboard. Daily lime and lemon juice and sugar was compulsory. One of the lads said the most frequent routine of the day was:

Breakfast: Coffee with hard biscuit and margarine and no milk.
Dinner: Soup, meat boiled in soup and spuds.
Tea: Tea with no milk, hard biscuit and margarine.
Supper: Tea and coffee made in separate kettles.

Trying to understand how this food was cooked was a problem. I'd noticed that on the *Rowland Evans* ship's register, there was 'no galley'. John Collins, archivist of Wivenhoe's Nottage Institute, explained to me:

Cooking was often done on the open deck. In fact, a temporary shelter which, not being part of the ship, was not included in the official tonnage figures and therefore not charged for! In fact, it was probably as strong as any integral structure that may have been provided instead, and less vulnerable in case of fire.

Almost like a kind of barbeque, therefore. There was nearly always a cook aboard the *Rowland Evans*. They had little training and often justified their employment by acting as stewards as well, which meant keeping the captain's quarters tidy.

The fact that officially John Evans declared 'NO GROG' in large letters on all his entries may seem comic to us now. It seems to accentuate the image of Captain Evans, with his stern Nonconformist conscience, as a forbidding figure. In fact, it was a common response in the 1850s. T. Spencer Wells, an adviser on nautical routine, maintained that abstinence 'is now carried into practice in a very considerable part of the merchant service in this county'.

Discipline had to be very strict when men were shut up together for months at a time. Experience might well have made captains only too aware that drunkenness could make for violence and so endanger life aboard ship. Not to mention that no drunken sailor could survive dangling off the rigging in a gale. Only once was there a voyage when John Evans allowed grog – a trip to South America in 1873.

The crew lists make it clear how discipline was to be administered. Men were left in no doubt what kind of behaviour was expected of them, and what happened when they broke the rules. Fines were given out. There was no flogging, but trouble most often arose when the ship was in harbour; then the British consul could be called upon to put men in jail. The most usual punishments for smaller offences, however, were small fines:

Fines for men on the *Rowland Evans*
Striking or assaulting any person on board: 5 shillings
Bringing or having on board spirituous liquids: 5 shillings
Drunkenness – first offence: 5 shillings
Drunkenness – second offence: 10 shillings
Taking on board and keeping possession of any firearms,
    knuckle duster, loaded cane, sling-shot, sword stick, bowie

knife, dagger or any other offensive knives without the concurrence of the master for every day which a seaman retains such weapon or instrument: 5 shillings

There was another list of 'unacceptable behaviour'. There were fines for such things as being late on board, being insolent to the captain or the mate, striking anybody aboard the ship, swearing, sleeping while on look-out, smoking below decks, neglecting to air bedding when ordered to, not attending divine service on Sundays, not being shaved and washed on Sunday, secreting contraband goods, or destroying a copy of the agreement. Disobedience to the captain could mean a month's imprisonment. Captain Evans was especially sensitive to insults and swearing from the crew.

A great help in keeping discipline was the fact that Captain John Evans was so tall with those magnificent mutton-chop whiskers. It certainly gave him an air of authority. He had learnt how to handle men from his father and grandfather's experiences as master mariners.

Flogging did not appear to be a disciplinary method among merchant seamen. In the case of extreme violence, men could be put in irons. There was a set rate of fines for certain transgressions, but Captain Evans seems mostly to have called upon the support of local British consuls to put men in jail when they were in port. Other possible punishments could be a deduction in their wages or dismissal.

Most crew chose to desert if they felt trouble coming. There were usually one or two desertions per voyage, which was the average for the time. There was gossip that some men deserted their ships to spend time with dusky beauties. More likely, desertions were opportunities to start new lives in a better economic situations, especially in America. It was not unusual for men to sign on and then not turn up when the ship sailed for home.

The captain seemed more at ease with younger sailors. On a trip to Barbados in 1867 nearly all the crew were in their 20s. His sister-in-law's son, Thomas Pryse, sailed with him often, and his own 17-year-old son William was aboard in 1875 for his first voyage. In 1879, at the age of 21, William was bosun on the *Rowland Evans*. This may well have made John Evans more understanding of younger men's needs, or of course they might have been more obedient and certainly fitter to withstand the physical demands of a long voyage. Few men were older than 40 on board, and they were usually the more difficult members of the crew and found the physical labour harder.

The captain cared for his crew's welfare too, so he had to make sure he had a well equipped medicine chest. It was a legal obligation. There appears little evidence of sickness on the *Rowland Evans*. A man was put in quarantine in Lisbon on the 1866 voyage, but there is no mention of what ailed him. A man went to hospital in Barbados in 1868, and in 1876 one man left the ship due to sickness in Cádiz.

As noted, Captain Evans' mates were usually Borth men, or at least they were Welsh. He did once have a Cornish mate. Mates were usually in their 20s. They really needed to be physically strong enough to man the sails, as it was usually the mate who gave commands from high up in the rigging. Most men had started their lives at sea at 16. At one time they got their position as mates from their reputation amongst the other men, but increasingly after 1850 they tended to need a Board of Trade certificate to become a mate.

After the mate came those who were called 'idlers', because they did not have to keep watch and they received higher wages. On larger ships, this could be the bosun, the carpenter, sail maker or cook. On the *Rowland Evans* there was usually only a cook and a bosun who could be classed as idlers.

The able seamen and the ordinary seamen did the bulk

of the work. Able seamen were men who had at least three years' experience at sea and were competent at the helm. They also had the advantage over the ordinary seaman in that they could have the pick of berths and food. They slept in the fo'c'sle in a narrow bunk or hammock, with a sea chest for their personal belongings. The accommodation though was cramped. As noted, only the captain had his own cabin, which he could share with his wife and family when they joined him.

The choice of crew

On the crew list the sailors noted their names or put a cross. They also gave the town where they were born, their age, qualifications, previous ship, the date they were discharged, the reason for their discharge, and what they earned per month. At every place they stopped, the British consul reported on anything which had happened to the crew that ought to be recorded, like desertions or lengthy illnesses. This was a legal obligation because it would be the basis of how to calculate men's pay.

On an early voyage in 1865, it seems that Captain John Evans took a crew of Borth men, except for the steward who came from Holyhead. After 1865 he did not have a large number of Borth men aboard, or even very many Welshmen, except on the shorter journeys. Only a trip, from Swansea to Bristol via Lisbon in 1866, had a crew who were entirely Welsh.

He found that using men from whatever part of the world he was sailing to gave him an edge in providing local knowledge. He had a special respect for Swedish sailors. There was at least one on every voyage. Captain Evans was more at ease in speaking and writing English than many other Borth captains, and of course there was the problem of coping with crews chosen from a wide variety of nationalities.

Sample of a typical crew list: Voyage commenced 29 April 1870, Rotterdam; terminated 12 December 1870, Bristol.

Name	Age	Birthplace	Capacity	Wage per calendar month
John Evans	41	Borth	Master	£4.10
David Davis	34	Borth	Mate	£3.50
Thomas Pryse	25	Borth	Bosun	£3.50
A. Matson	27	Sweden	Cook and steward	£3.00
A. Evans	21	Caernarvon	AB	£2.10
John Williams	27	Lisbon	AB	£2.10
William Jackson	25	Manchester	AB	£2.10
Joseph R. Organ	18	Charleston	os	Did not join
Robert McCrae	33	Stornaway	AB	Deserted
William Dinnun	21	York	os	£2.10

An interesting feature of this crew list is that the clerk filled in the front page and added that it was agreed there should be no profane language on board. The British consul at Montevideo, where the ship anchored from 23 July to 18 August 1870, declared, 'I hereby certify that Robert McCrae has been left behind on the grounds of desertion and that I have inquired into the matter and find the allegation to be correct and that a proper entry in the official log book has been produced to me.' The ship went on to Buenos Aires, arriving there on 23 August and leaving on 23 September, with a new crew member, a William Dinnun, from an American ship.

John Evans' attitude to his superiors seems curious. He was aware that he should report any problems quickly, but he found keeping paperwork in order difficult. He declares in January 1871:

> Sir,
> The superintendent, having called my attention to my making the entries in my official log book in the wrong place, I beg to say that I regret the same and I will be more careful in future.

Little did he know what a reputation he was to acquire with his log books later.

CHAPTER 15

Mice and cockroaches ate my log book!

SEARCHING FOR THE crew lists, Peter and I had read the log book's tiny print and columns of facts. Working our way through blue folders of the Aberystwyth Shipping Records, Peter found a series of letters about one of the 'worthy' captain's missing log books.

His explanation, when he could not produce his log book in Bristol in 1880, on his way back from Buenos Aires, was certainly original. Apparently, mice and cockroaches ate his log book!

It's very striking that the immediate reaction of the captain's letter is one of confidence, both in the handwriting and the tone of the letter. Legal advice must have been taken in order to produce this kind of language; it's incredibly florid and he seems determined to be impressive by using a formal style. He certainly does not seem like a man overawed by authority.

His letter reads:

I, John Evans, Master of the brig *Rowland Evans* of Aberystwyth, do solemnly declare that the mice and cockroaches ate my log book on the voyage home from Paysandu and that I was unable to produce it to the shipping master at the port of Bristol and do make the solemn declaration conscientiously believing the same to be true and by virtue of an act made and passed in the sixth year of the reign of his late Majesty King William the Fourth institute, an act to repeal an act of the present session of Parliament institute, an Act for the more effectual abolition of Oaths and Affirmation in lieu, therefore for the entire suppression of voluntary extra judicial oaths and affivadi and to make other provisions for the abolition of unnecessary oaths,

I am, Sir, Your obedient servant

John Evans

Master of the *Rowland Evans*

Declared before me this 20 June 1880

Pickick magistrate of Bristol.

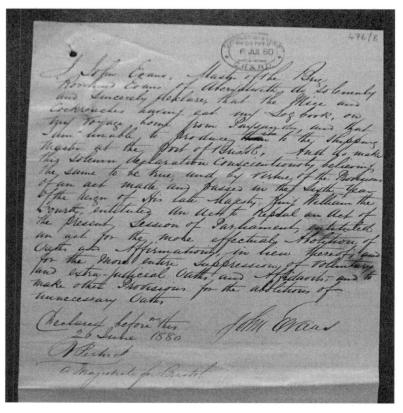

John Evans' explanation of what had happened to his log book.

We know that we are dealing here with a man who is clearly uncomfortable doing things 'by the book'. Is this his problem? The language is so cumbersome.

The incident seems to have inspired an incredible flurry of pompous letters. Obviously, an invasion of mice and cockroaches had to be taken very seriously.

General Register & Record Office of Shipping and Seamen
82 Basinghall Street
London E.C.

To The Superintendent
Mercantile Marine Office
Bristol

Re: *Rowland Evans*

It would have been desirable had you reported whether any confirmation of the Master's statement with reference to the destruction of the Official Log could be obtained from the Mate, or any other member of the Crew. I presume that at least it would have been ascertained whether the ship was infested with Mice and Cockroaches to the extent implied.

Robert Jackson
Reg Gen
29 June 1880

This letter got a prompt reaction.

The Superintendent
Bristol

I have seen John James (one of the crew) who lives forward & he states he has only seen one or two mice & a few cockroaches, he has had nothing destroyed. I have seen the Mate alongside the ship; he stated he did not know what had become of the Log Book; he could not tell whether he had signed any entry in the Log Book since his arrival in this port or not: he stated he could not say nothing [*sic*] more than this. I then called the Master & in the presence of both I told the Master what the Mate said.

The Master replied, 'I can say he has not signed anything' & then said to the Mate, 'Have you signed any entry in the Log since we arrived in Falmouth or Bristol?' The Mate answered 'No'. I asked the Mate for his explanation of this prevarication & he could give me none; after suggestions from the Master he stated he did not understand my questions. I told the Master we could not send a favourable report. The Master, however, said he could not help it that he had stated the truth. The Mate appears to be a shuffling Welshman & because he did not know what the Master had said he could not say anything.

T. Porteous 30:6:80

Sir,
The Foregoing is forwarded for your information.
G. Whitwill
Supt.

'Shuffling' Welshmen obviously cannot be trusted. It seems the poor mate had trouble understanding English. It does not give a very favorable impression of the English official.

The Registrar General of Seamen
London

To the Superintendent
Merchant Marine Office
Bristol

The Master's explanation is most unsatisfactory; it appears highly improbable that a document which is in frequent use during a voyage could have been destroyed in the manner described and without a particle remaining. A decision in the Case cannot be given at present, but in the meantime, in order not to detain the Ship, BB may be granted upon the Master depositing the sum of £2.

Robert Jackson
The Registrar General of Seamen
B.B. has been granted on deposit of 40/-

The formal letter from the Register General explains the error that the captain committed. Not reporting a desertion and then replacing him without noting it on the crew list was obviously illegal. Another letter finalises the case of the 'black books' (where misdeeds were recorded). Officials do not seem to have a very shrewd perception of character, perhaps a feeling that the Welsh are not overly bright!

The next letter is from the mercantile marine office.

I beg to forward herewith the statutory declaration of the master of the *Rowland Evans* of Aberystwyth, who has just arrived at this port, that his official log book has been eaten by mice and cockroaches. The Articles List C (to show the characters of crew) are forwarded herewith, together with the master's explanation respecting the desertion of one of his crew at Paysandu not being endorsed and his shipping a man at Buenos Aires without the sanction of the council. The BB is withheld awaiting your instructions.

28 June 1880

It seems strange to us that an explanation like, 'the mice and cockroaches ate my log book' should be examined so solemnly. Surely, as unconvincing as a child's explanation of 'the dog who ate my homework'? The captain had little respect for updating the 'log', although he must surely have realised it was a legal obligation. John Evans was not backward in coming forward to defend himself.

CHAPTER 16

The demon drink

A SHIP WHICH carried more than 50 people aboard had to have a doctor. Both the captain and doctor had to keep records about the health of passengers and crew. The Mercantile Marine Act insisted that the captain was obliged to keep an official log recording illness, births and deaths on board, any misconduct, desertion and punishment and a description of each man's conduct. The description of a man's conduct was simply written as good or very good, but examples of misconduct were gone into in detail, and in his early days on the brig these seem to have driven the captain into bouts of temper.

Log books needed to be deposited after each foreign voyage, or half-yearly if doing home trade. Any misconduct noted the date and hour of its occurrence, the place where it happened, and the fine or forfeiture inflicted, as required by Act of Parliament. This often caused Borth master mariners problems if they were not fluent in English. Many such captains spoke and wrote English as a second language. Captain Evans seemed very fluent in both languages and the language used aboard ship was most likely to be English.

As an historical source, the log books for the *Rowland Evans* lack much detail. Dates are confused or missing. Merchant ships filled in only a few pages for each voyage. The logs of the Royal Navy were much more detailed. Masters or captains kept meticulous records each week of ships' locations, movements, the weather, signals, orders carried out, the punishments, duties and tasks of men. There were even fuller records from the doctors, or scientists aboard exploration ships. Captain Evans had other obligations as a merchant seaman, and had not been trained in the same way in his approach to paper work.

As soon as the *Rowland Evans* reached shore, men were free to do as they wished. The demon drink took hold and lovely ladies were encountered. Months of living together as monks must inevitably have erupted into problems when they got ashore.

As an example, on the 1867 voyage of the *Rowland Evans* to Barbados, a drunken cook returned aboard to find an angry mate waiting for him. Joseph the cook, from Liverpool, was accused of defrauding men of their butter and four grams of tea. The cook did not care. He went ashore and got even more drunk, which did not sweeten his temper. The mate was not best pleased either, as he had to make his own meal! He reproved the cook and the captain appeared. The cook stomped off, muttering that he did not care for 'the damned captain or the bloody ship'. He was not alarmed when he was threatened with being taken to the British consul, which usually meant being put in jail for the night.

Cooks seemed to be a problem. Sailors often said, 'The Lord sent us the grub but the devil sent us the cook!' On 15 May 1868, at Berbice, another cook used insulting language towards the captain. The cook refused to work and the captain refused to give him his discharge. Tempers flared. The cook threatened to become violent if he was left aboard ship. His punishment was being sent to jail and he was given 14 days hard labour. The captain had had enough of the man by now, and did in fact discharge him. At the same time, another man was discharged for being drunk and disorderly at Berbice. Obviously, the heat was getting to them, as the boatswain also was actually discharged by mutual consent.

On the next voyage, 20-year-old Hector, who was serving on the voyage to Berbice as a cook, was handled more tactfully. The young man had an exotic background. He came from Demerara, which is part of the old Dutch colony which became British Guyana – it's a part of the world with a turbulent history of slave rebellions. Even after the British stopped the slave trade, there was a volatile combination of races, Dutch, Creoles, the British and Africans from Rio de Janeiro.

Mate John Simon thought that Hector was unwilling to do his work as a cook. He was told that, in that case, he would serve as an able bodied seaman instead, and another native of Berbice, James Lowbartus, was to be the cook and steward. Hector, however, must have wished that he stayed as a cook when he made the unpleasant discovery that as an able bodied seaman he was expected to unfurl the fore topgallant sail. He refused to do so, as he claimed that he was not aboard ship to go aloft.

Where the above is noted in the log book, the captain seems to have been very angry. One of the men got intoxicated and had called him 'a damned Welshman and a bloody son of a bitch'. The man had also stripped off his shirt and seemed ready for a fight. Unfortunately, as the writing is difficult to read here, a cross has been drawn through the page. The 'worthy captain' may have been embarrassed seeing swear words, at his expense, written down for all to see. He may not have wanted the incident recorded at all. Maybe he was embarrassed that his own temper was getting the better of him.

There were times, however, when Captain Evans showed a fatherly approach to the younger seamen. Twenty-two-year-old Canadian, John Allen, turned up for duty on 13 April 1869, but did not do any work because there was no one there to tell him what to do. A policeman took him to the consul, and he was put in prison for the night. The next day, on his return to the ship, the poor young man was found to be suffering from a looseness of the bowels, and he was given arrowroot and kept on a light diet and given proper medicine until he got better.

The captain didn't take such kind a view of another drunk, Peter Lecondica, who used very bad language to the mate, the boatswain and John Allen, calling them the 'sons of whores' and striking out at other members of the crew. His punishment was to lose three days' pay.

Not all the misdemeanours were fully recorded. On a voyage in 1868, a member of the crew was imprisoned in Constantinople. What had he done? Was he ever released?

Drink certainly seemed to do strange things to men's minds. In 1875, William German was drunk and left the ship without signing his release, so received no pay. More detailed records of a deceased seaman, in September 1875, do not seem to have survived, but it's unlikely there was anything sinister about it.

I found a note from the British consul at Buenos Aires about the fate of a seaman from Hamburg called H. Wagner. The captain had applied external liniments to him when he first became sick with rheumatism. The man was only 29.

I hereby certify that the within named H. Wagner has been discharged and left behind at this port, on the alleged ground of rheumatism. I have enquired into the matter and find that the allegation is true and the grounds sufficient that I have accordingly granted my sanction to his being so left and that his wages as follows have been paid to me and his effects delivered.

Paid in cash to Consul for H. Wagner, balance due to him up to 3/4/71 was £2.10.6. Effects: one bag.

'Effects: one bag'; how long did he survive after this? Again, it seems rather careless of the captain not to have reported the German's sickness earlier, although he sounds more genuinely apologetic this time.

The later log books were in a simpler format, and the captain seems to have had a better control of his temper. It might have something to do with the fact that the earlier voyages were in hotter climes, which explains why tempers flared so easily. It's also noticeable that there seemed to be bad feeling about the Welsh, especially among the Liverpool sailors.

Events aboard the *Rowland Evans*, 1865–76

Date	Special Events	Sickness and Desertion	Discipline Problems and punishments
1865	John Evans of Morben is the owner.		T. Jones discharged
1866 July	Owner changes to Captain Evans. Thomas Pryse, his nephew, joins.	Man put in quarantine. Hurst of Liverpool deserts.	Drunken cook defrauded men of tea and butter. Cook J. Williams from Liverpool in prison in Constantinople.
1868 February		James Herbert has two visits to hospital. James Rolls has one visit to hospital. Man discharged at Berbice by mutual consent.	Cook Alfred Loris refused duty, threatening to be dangerous, sent to jail and given 14 days hard labour and discharged. Man discharged for being drunk and disorderly at Berbice. Discharged men given back pay. Hector Dawson refuses to work then made to be A.B., calls the captain but won't climb the rigging. Drunken sailor calls captain a 'damn Welshman'.
1869		Frenchman deserts, Canadian confused by where to report and treated for sickness of the bowels.	Frenchman insults officers as 'sons of whores' and disobeys. Loses three days' pay.
1870	The captain admits he has been keeping his entries in the wrong place in his log book.	One man never joined. Robert McCrae deserted at Montevideo.	
1871	Captain apologies for not recording Wagner's discharge on grounds of rheumatism in the log book.	James Making of Liverpool deserted at Rosario after serving only two months.	Wagner treated for rheumatism by applying external liniments.
1871–2		Deserted negro at Uruguay. One man died.	

1873–4		One man deserted at Concepción.	
1874	Grog allowed!		
1875		One man left drunk without signing his release.	Another man left without signing release.
1875–6	Son William joins as A.B at age of 17.	Norwegian left at Montevideo.	
1877	New owner, Morgan Owen of Aberystwyth.	Very young Norwegian left at Montevideo.	
1878		Two men deserted. Sale of cargo by auction.	
1879		William Evans, bosun at age of 21.	

CHAPTER 17

The *Rowland Evans'* last voyage

CAPTAIN JOHN EVANS had a very successful career with the *Rowland Evans* and the ship was widely admired. Then, suddenly, on the last journey everything fell apart. Even from the very beginning something was amiss. The vessel was plunging into further difficulties. The crew list is on page 127.

An incident reported by the *Aberystwyth Observer*, 22 January 1881, based on a telegram from *Pemambro*, states: '*Rowland Evans* of Aberystwyth (Captain Evans, Borth) from Natal for New York and the *Mary Eddy* have been in collision. The former grounded and had to lighten to get off. The extent of injuries was not known.'

Even for the signing on of the crew, things did not seem to follow the usual pattern. There was the usual variety of young men of varying nationalities, a Swedish sailor, a Norwegian, an Irishman and a Londoner, but also four Borth men were sailing and a man from Aberystwyth, and also an elderly man from Cardiff.

The troubles began in New York. Three Borth men and a Swedish sailor deserted. They included the mate, the cook and the bosun, which cannot have pleased the captain very much. After all, getting a passage to New York was a stroke of luck for men determined to start a life in the New World. This was often the first step for men with ambitions to leave their native

Name	Place of origin	Age	Status	Date of discharge	Reason for Discharge
John Evans	Borth	51	Master		
David Hughes	Borth	26	Mate	17 November 1880	Deserted
David Davies	Borth	29	Cook and steward	April 1881, New York	Deserted
Lewis Jenkins	Borth	23	Bosun	April 1881, New York	Deserted
John James	Borth	17	AB	26 July 1882, Antwerp	Discharged
Svend Gjesdaahysdahl	Norway	43	AB	1 February 1881, Rio Grande	Sickness. Left behind at hospital.
Oscar Jacobson	Sweden	19	AB	April 1881, New York	Deserted
George Davies	Fishguard	21	Carpenter. First ship	12 August 1882, Antwerp	Discharged
George Nicholas	Greece	31	AB	Signed on at Rio Grande.	Did not join. James Powell took his place.
James Powell	Cardiff	46	AB. First ship	April 1881, New York	Deserted
Enoch Morgan	Aberystwyth	40	AB. Joined at New York.	26 July 1882, Antwerp	Discharged
Christopher Davenish	Galway	40	Chief mate. Joined at New York.	February 1882	Discharged by mutual consent.
Herbert Symonds	London	28	Cook and steward. Joined at New York.	26 July 1882, Antwerp	Discharged
Thomas R. Owen	Liverpool	19	OS	26 July 1882, Antwerp	Discharged
Fleck	Germany	28	OS	26 July 1882, Antwerp	Discharged
Jenkin Jones	Aberaeron		Mate	26 July 1882, Antwerp	Discharged

country. The British Consul did not seem concerned by the desertions. He immediately approved the hiring of five more men.

At Rio Grande, Brazil, other problems arose. James Powell of Cardiff's case is strange, as he was 46 and on his *first* ship. Apparently, he replaced a Greek sailor who had signed on, but never joined the ship. No wonder Powell deserted. Life on board a sailing ship would have been a shock to the inexperienced, especially an older man, for this was a physically demanding life.

Another older sailor, a Norwegian aged 43, had to be left at the hospital at Rio Grande. The British Consul in Rio Grande said, 'it was on account of sickness and inability to proceed on the voyage according to the doctor's certificate, and the balance of his wages £13-11-2 had been delivered to this office.'

In Montevideo, Christopher Davenish, a 40-year-old Irish sailor, left by mutual consent with his clothes and the balance of his wages paid in cash in the captain's presence. He had taken the place of the mate who had deserted in New York, so now John Evans had to look for yet another mate.

Fortunately, he found 24-year-old Jenkin Jones from Aberaeron. Jenkin was more likely to get on with the master. In fact, he was the only one to stay on board for the last leg of the voyage – the trip from Antwerp to Wales. None of the rest of the crew stayed on after Antwerp, although the crew list for September 1882 was said to be a continuation of the original agreement made in Cardiff in 1880. Had the men left because they had doubts about the captain or the state of the ship? They certainly would not have enjoyed unloading the cargo. It was very heavy work. Young John James of Borth and the carpenter from Fishguard were quick to leave, as were all the men who had joined the ship at New York.

CHAPTER 18

Antwerp

THE NEXT STAGE of the voyage was meant to end in Falmouth, and then the ship was to sail on to Antwerp. Antwerp was not popular with young Welsh sailors. In my Aunty Get's collection of postcards was a postcard of the Brabo Fountain in Antwerp. It appears to have been sent by one of the local sailors about to sail for Cuba. His opinion of Antwerp was: 'it was not much of a place; all the people spend their time in cafés or some such place. On Saturday night you may meet dozens of drunken men.'

As noted, Captain Evans doesn't seem to have brought much home from foreign ports, suggesting that it was the ships he loved and the mechanics of sailing rather than being exposed to different ways of life and cultures.

I would love to see all the places that my great-grandfather visited. Visiting Antwerp might give clues about the ship's last journey. Would there be glimpses of ghosts past along the riverbank and in the hidden alleyways and courtyards of the older parts of the city? If I visited, would I come to an understanding of what was troubling the captain?

I wondered what Sarah might have made of this foreign city. Unlike a lot of captains' wives from Borth, as noted, Sarah chose not to go on long journeys with her husband. She certainly did not have the stamina of one Borth lady, who gave birth at sea and gave her son the wonderful name of John

'Seaborn' Evans. Many Borth women were accustomed to earning a living in strenuous fashions, like hauling peat into Aberystwyth or finding cockles in Ynyslas.

Sarah's life would have been more ladylike. She could not have stomached the smell of the cargoes on the *Rowland Evans*, nor the clamour of men shouting. The possibility of taking the entire family, as other captains did, was not for the Evans family. They were too genteel, except for the dashing son, William. The daughters loved their home too much to want to be on the move.

In a faded photograph of Sarah in her finery, it shows her looking rather anxious. She seems refined with her lace caps, large brooches and a fan. It would be understandable that she would prefer to meet up with her husband at Continental ports during his brief time ashore, rather than endure cramped conditions on those long, hot voyages to South America.

Why did John Evans choose to travel to South America so often? The cargoes probably were more profitable. There may also have been more than economic necessity driving him on. But he must also have nursed a deep passion for seafaring that kept him on a relentless cycle of voyages.

For Sarah, those times she spent with her husband in Continental cities must have been special. She probably enjoyed shopping. On my visit to Antwerp I saw quaint shops which sold fine hand-made lace. Lace was something highly treasured by Victorian women. I remember my grandmother showing me her precious Belgian lace scarf that she kept in an embroidered satin-lined bag.

The kind of food served at Antwerp restaurants would have been to Sarah's taste too – wholesome Flemish food like shrimps, rabbit and duck from those meadows that Rubens and Brueghel painted. It's harder to imagine what Sarah would have made of the religious art of the Catholic churches. Being used to plain Welsh chapels, I suspect she would have felt uncomfortable had she entered the wonderful Gothic cathedral of Our Lady that dominates Antwerp.

She and John would, however, have walked to the Grote Markt to see the magnificent Town Hall and beautiful sixteenth-century guild houses clustered around the statue of Antwerp's hero, Silvius Brabo. This statue, of a strong muscular man, is throwing a dismembered hand into the air. The legend of Silvius Brabo would have had an obvious appeal to John Evans. Brabo is said to have cut off the hand of the mighty giant Antigone and thrown it into the River Scheldt. It was the giant's punishment for the way he treated sailors who could not pay their tolls.

Like other visitors, John and Sarah may have ambled from the square to the river itself to see the oldest building in Antwerp, a fairytale-looking building called the Het Steen with its romantic turrets. Standing in front of the fortress was a statue of yet another grotesquely outsized man, standing menacingly over two small people. He is known as the Teaser of Antwerp. Apparently, he would wander the streets at night, growing bigger and bigger, and that would terrify the drunks away.

The Scheldt, like so many rivers that run through modern cities, is now becoming a centre for tourism. Old warehouses are changing into fashionable apartments and boutiques, and the jumble of buildings along the riverbank includes odd mixtures of old and modern creations, like Richard Rogers' Law Courts, with its strange wing-like formations. Most shipping sails right into the docks, with its forest of cranes, or line up along the riverbank.

I wanted to imagine how nineteenth-century ships would have looked. I had the good fortune of meeting a helpful assistant in a second-hand bookshop. She found me some Dutch-language books which gave me a real insight into the days of sail. Along with marvellously evocative photographs, there was text by a famous Flemish writer, Hubert Lampo.

The book showed Antwerp in the 1880s, heaving with traders. Even in the main shopping streets, country women came to sell their produce, and cows walked to market, driven by peasants in voluminous smocks. Women, wrapped up in warm woolly shawls and serge skirts with aprons, either chatted away or waited for custom. Gentleman in bowler hats escorted their wives in floral bonnets and silk-caped dresses around an array of large wicker baskets with goods laid out to sell. Dotted around the city were workshops where men made articles needed by merchants in the days of sail – barrels, ropes and chains.

Down by the river, rows and rows of carts with their patient dray horses waited to be unloaded. Men rolled barrel after barrel. Bricks and timber were stacked high along the edge of the riverbank. One local Antwerp historian said, 'one must first have looked at this forest of masts, packed closely together, extending as far as the eyes can see, and experienced the intense interest with which the population regards the grand sailing ships, before understanding the real significance of Antwerp as a commercial town; a world of trading interests, rough, hungry for wealth, strong and dynamic.' All sizes of boat plied their trade up the river, and a continual flow of people came to watch their comings and goings.

A statute by Constantin Meurier of a muscular docker is typical of the men whose unending tramp of feet over the narrow springy gang planks was slowed down by the heavy burden of sacks of grain. Ironically, when Alderman Van der Taelen wanted to introduce pneumatic elevators in 1883, 3,000 dock workers protested and there were bloody riots. Warehouse after warehouse regurgitated cargo, and narrow alleyways opened to courtyards filling with debris, both material and human. Old medieval buildings opened into sinister alleyways where anything could happen.

An English book gave me an idea of Antwerp's commercial importance. The chief imports were coffee, cotton, salted hides, rice, wool, cereals, oilseed and Norwegian timber. Exports were of fine textiles for the South and Central American markets, wrought iron, worked copper, paper, cut glass, furniture. In 1883, 663 sailing ships and 3,700 steamships called at the port.

Captain Evans must have explored these docks, wondering about his next cargo and crew. He must also have wondered about the future of sail with so many steamships arriving. Depressed by his most recent voyage, which had taken him from Cardiff to South America, there seems to have been a strong element of discontent aboard his ship.

September 1882: At Antwerp, half-yearly agreement on account of being for home trade only.

Name	Age	Place of Origin	Status	Discharged
William Lowe	20	Liverpool	AB	Discharged. Vessel lost.
Lars John Neilsen	19	Norway	AB	Never joined
Karl Kristensen	20	Dromon?	AB	Never joined
John Welsh	30	Liverpool	AB	Discharged
John Fletcher	39	Liverpool	AB	Discharged
Richard Mayne	40	London	AB	Flushing. Deserted
Joseph Mannoest	42	Durquey	AB	Discharged
Martin De Groulon		Antwerp		Discharged

The captain stayed in Antwerp for just under two months, and in that time he found a cargo of silver sand and a new crew. They mainly seemed to be English, from Liverpool, and older than most of his usual crew. The mate was Welsh.

The suggestion that the ship itself needed attention is seen in an advertisement from the *Shipping and Mercantile Gazette*, Friday, 28 July 1882. The *Rowland Evans* was put up for sale, but did not find a buyer.

A complete lack of confidence in future ventures is clear. Two Norwegians sign on, but do not join the ship when it leaves Antwerp. This very much had the feeling of a scratch crew. Had John Evans resorted to using a crimper to find his crew, or did he find them idling about the docks? They certainly were unlikely to have much loyalty to him. The ship's register noted that it had sunk off Bardsey Island. My great-aunts and grandma had told me that the crew, Sarah and the captain had returned to Borth in rowing boats after the ship had sunk. But how did it become a disciplinary matter for the captain?

Terry Davies gives a clue in his book, *Borth: A Maritime History*. There had been a Court of Inquiry, with the judgement noting that this was the clearest case of abandonment that the court had ever come across. As a result, the captain lost his master's certificate for a year. But what cycle of events brought that about?

PART IV

The Final Disgrace

CHAPTER 19

Read all about it!

THE GREAT DRAMA of Captain Evans' life happened on 12 September 1882. The *Rowland Evans* sank off the Welsh coast on its way home from Antwerp. There was no gale, no mighty storm, as my relatives had described to me. Could there have been some other force of nature? On 6 October, Captain Evans was brought in front of a Board of Trade disciplinary hearing in connection with the sinking.

A deep sea diver in north Wales, Chris Holden, explained how I might find out more about the ship's last days. Local newspaper accounts of Welsh shipping wrecks are to be found on microfilm in archives. Searching through microfilm is time-consuming. He was kind enough to trawl through Welsh newspapers of the time.

I clung on to the hope that the loss of the ship might have simply been as a result of the physical deterioration of the vessel. The *Rowland Evans* was 18 years old, and during that time she had carried heavy cargoes over considerable distances. Most ships of this type were expected to last for 20 years but, obviously, this ship was not in the best of shape. There had been an earlier, brief, visit to South Shields for repairs. Later, when she left for South America on 21 July 1880, she carried a carpenter, George Davies of Fishguard, so there had been anxieties about her seaworthiness earlier.

When the ship arrived at Falmouth in September 1882,

it became obvious that there was trouble with the pumps. A change of crew at the next port of call, Antwerp, compounded that difficulty.

Chris' searches revealed some intriguing information. One of the clearest accounts was in three instalments in the *Western Mail*.

Western Mail (Cardiff) Friday, 6 October 1882

Mr J.C. Fowler, the Swansea Stipendiary, assisted by captains Beazley and Harland, nautical assessors, opened a Board of Trade inquiry into the abandonment of the ship *Rowland Evans*, which took place on the 11th of September, about five miles from the Cardigan Lightship. Mr Strick appeared for the Board of Trade, and Mr Lawrence for the owners, captain and mate. John Evans, the master, owned 36 shares out of a total of 64 shares in the vessel, which were mortgaged for £600. The vessel was insured for £1,800.

She left Falmouth for Antwerp with a cargo of 253 tons of hides. While she was in the former place, she made five or six inches of water in an hour, and while in the dock at the latter place, she made about 9 inches every twelve hours. She left Antwerp with a cargo of silver sand, and shortly afterwards sprung a leak, which could not be reached easily internally. The pumps were worked for some time, but ultimately they became choked with sand. The master, seeing the ship in imminent danger of sinking, got ready the boat and left her, taking his wife and the crew, which consisted of seven hands. They stayed by the ship for some time, and as she did not go down, they returned to her, and cut two holes in the deck in order to sink her out of the way of other navigation. A few hours afterwards, the boat reached Borth, Cardiganshire, which, strange to say, was in front of the captain's home. The log and the captain's instruments and charts and clothes were left behind. Examined by Mr Strick, the captain said there was no port which the vessel could have reached in her condition, and he was afraid she would go down with all hands if he stayed on board any longer. The inquiry was adjourned until today (Friday).

So was the captain making a sensible decision? The ship was thought to be sinking. When it appeared to be slow to sink, he thought it best to hasten the sinking to get it out of the way of other shipping speedily, by making holes in the vessel. Was that the right thing for a captain to do?

Western Mail (Cardiff) Monday, 9 October 1882

BOARD OF INQUIRY AT SWANSEA

The Board of Trade inquiry into the abandonment of the *Rowland Evans* in Cardigan Bay was resumed on Saturday, when two other witnesses were called who contradicted the captain and the mate and corroborated evidence given by the other members of the crew. The captain, who was recalled, said that after they landed at Borth, the men asked him for money. Having paid them what was due to them, he refused to give them any more and then they threatened to make him sorry for it. The men came into court again and swore there was no truth in this statement.

Mr Lawrence, in addressing the court for the captain, said his client may have committed an error of judgement in leaving the ship when he did, but it was ridiculous to suppose he had scuttled her, which was what the crew had tried to make out. That the boat had landed at the captain's house was merely a strange coincidence. Mr Strict, for the Board of Trade, asked the court whether the master had made any attempt to take his vessel into a place of safety and whether he had prematurely abandoned her. The court then adjourned until noon today, when the decision will be given.

Such a surly crew! Despite their efforts to give the impression that the captain had scuttled the ship, it became obvious their manner had undermined their trustworthiness as witnesses, especially after the scene in front of the house. Yet, was the captain in too much of a rush to abandon the ship?

Western Mail (Cardiff) Tuesday, 10 October 1882

THE ABANDONMENT OF THE *ROWLAND EVANS*
– SUSPENSION OF THE CAPTAIN'S CERTIFICATE – THE
MATE CENSURED

Mr Fowler, in giving the decision of the court, said this was the clearest example of premature abandonment which had ever come under his notice. The vessel was abandoned in fine weather, with a calm sea and a favourable breeze, with every spar and sail intact, with two excellent boats, a pump still throwing water, with an obedient crew, and within 28 or 30 miles of the visible Cardiganshire coast, which offered two or three places that might have been approached with safety. The statement of the captain that she was sinking was incorrect. She was abandoned while a moral certainty remained of taking her into some port, and, considering the state of the wind and tide, it was even probable that if she had not been wilfully injured – if holes had not been cut in her deck, and her scupper pipes ripped open – she would have drifted ashore the following night. The captain had grievously failed to discharge the primary duty of a master, which was to cling to his vessel to the last, and never to abandon her except under pressure of immediate danger to life. The court had, therefore, decided to suspend his certificate for twelve calendar months, and to censure the mate for not protesting against the course taken by the master.

It was a humiliating verdict that he had grievously failed in his duty. That must have hurt a proud experienced master mariner. After all, Captain Evans seemed to have abandoned the ship because he thought the lives of his crew and wife *were* in danger. The crew could scarcely be considered to be totally reliable, and the ship was not in the best order. Did Captain Evans deserve so stern a judgement?

To some, he had deliberately scuppered the ship in order to get the insurance money, although it was never said explicitly. He would not have acquired *all* the insurance money, as he only owned 36 shares. There were rumours, not unknown among some Borth captains, that damaging a ship to get an insurance payment would give them a kind of 'pension' in old age. The *Cambrian News and Merionethshire Standard* had run articles about ships being over insured, especially in fine weather.

I'd become fond of John Evans as I worked on his story. He seemed, if anything, a man of great rectitude. Could I rescue his reputation?

I looked through all the newspaper references that Chris had given me, and they all said very much the same thing. The *Cambrian News*, a newspaper printed in Aberystwyth, did at least give witnesses' names and more detail of the crew's comments:

Charles Lowe, who acted as the boatswain, and Thomas Fletcher and Joseph Maneart, seamen, contradicted the captain and mate on some important points. All three agreed that one pump was used during the whole of the journey from Antwerp and, according to one of them, the ship did not take more water than could be pumped out by five or six strokes of the pump every half-hour until the night before the abandonment. They could not account for the vessel having sprung a leak and knew nothing about such a thing. They were all unanimous in saying that if they were as well acquainted with the coast as the captain, they would have taken the vessel into one of the ports on the Cardiganshire coast without taking any risk. One of the men said they landed from the boat right at the captain's front door.

Another newspaper, the *Aberystwyth Observer*, was the most informative about the crew's evidence:

On Saturday, Mr Strict called two other witnesses who contradicted the captain and mate and corroborated evidence given by the rest of the crew. The captain then said the men threatened to make him sorry because he refused them more money than was due to them, but the sailors who were recalled said this was not true.

CHAPTER 20

Further Surprises

TEN YEARS AFTER my initial approach to Chris Holden, he got in touch with me again. To my amazement he had found out more information about the *Rowland Evans*. He'd been asked by the Nautical Archaeological Society to write about some ships that had sunk in north Cardigan Bay, including the brig *Rowland Evans* abandoned in 'mysterious circumstances' in 1882.

He discovered that the ship had problems early on in its existence. According to the *Shipping and Mercantile Gazette*, 9 December 1869, it had apparently put into Palermo, Sicily, having lost its stanchions, bulwark boats, sails and ropes. The vessel had lain on its beam ends. However, for well over ten years afterwards, it seems to have made a prosperous living sailing to and from South America with no problems. But, as already noted, on 22 January 1881, according to the *Aberystwyth Observer*, a telegram had been sent to say that the *Rowland Evans* had collided with the *Mary Eddy* on a journey to New York. 'The former grounded and had to lighten to get off. The extent of injuries was not known.'

Chris also discovered that in July 1882 the ship was found to be leaky and had to jettison a portion of its cargo of hides in Falmouth.

Of course, the next port of call after Falmouth was Antwerp. It becomes clear that John Evans was a worried captain who would dearly love to sell his ship. It's obvious that the ship was no longer an attractive project, as no one offered to buy it. As noted, it was put up for sale in the *Shipping and Mercantile Gazette*, 28 July 1882. Then it set out for Garston, near Liverpool, with a cargo of silver sand.

As the ship passed Flushing (Vlissingen, some 50 miles west of Antwerp), it was discovered that it had to leave with the loss of an anchor. In fact, two anchors had to be replaced.

An account from the *Aberystwyth Observer*, 16 September 1882, gives added information:

WRECK OF AN ABERYSTWYTH VESSEL.
On Tuesday afternoon, Borth was aroused by the arrival, in a boat, of Captain Evans, of the brig *Rowland Evans*, and his crew, the captain being a native of the village. From the statements of the captain and crew it appears that the Rowland Evans was bound from Antwerp to Garston, near Liverpool, with a load of silver ore. The vessel had a beautiful passage, the run from Antwerp to the Irish Channel being made in three days. During the voyage the vessel leaked slightly, but no difficulty was experienced in keeping the water under control until about ten o'clock on Monday night, when it was found that it was gaining, and the pumps became choked with the fine ore. During the night the men were kept at the pumps, but in the morning the water had increased so much that it was decided to abandon the ship, and the long boat, with all on board, was steered for Borth, which place was reached at four o'clock in the afternoon. The vessel was abandoned twenty-five miles S.W. of Bardsey Island. After being provided with food, the crew were forwarded to Liverpool by the night mail. The vessel was owned by Mr John Evans (the captain) and others, and the vessel was insured in the Aberystwyth and Aberaeron Insurance Clubs for about £ 1,800. Her tonnage was 208.

This paper was the only one to mention the name of the insurance company of the ship.

Another account, from *The Cambrian* (Welsh Newspapers Online), gave an exceptionally detailed account; the first days of the Board of Trade hearing in the 6 October issue and the judgement in the 13 October issue. The accounts are more or less verbatim of the disciplinary hearing, with vast amounts of detail, if a little technical at times. The complete text is in an appendix at the back of the book.

From the accounts one thing is clear, the obvious problem came from the state of the ship's pumps, complicated by the fact that the captain and the mate had given their own version of what had happened, and that the crew had given another explanation.

The new Antwerp crew had not been aboard the ship when water was pumped out on the trip from Falmouth to Antwerp and the mate had said that the leaks seemed rather alarming – five to six inches of water per hour at Falmouth. And when the time came to leave Antwerp, a heavy cargo like silver sand could not have been helpful. The sand was fine and could easily have choked the pumps.

It's a fair comment from the Stipendiary to say that the captain should have repaired and overhauled the ship before it left Antwerp, so that both pumps were in good order. The desertion of able seaman Richard McGuire at Flushing is indicative that at least one member of the crew was losing faith in the ship's seaworthiness. The court considered the anchors to be in good order, because the anchors had been replaced at Flushing but the pumps continued to function badly up until midnight.

A bigger problem seems to have influenced the captain's decisions when they reached Cardigan Bay. Convinced that the leaks were endangering the ship, he ordered the ship be abandoned, with his wife and crew taken into to the long boat. When they looked back, the *Rowland Evans* did not seem to be sinking. The captain, however, seemed to think that it was inevitable it would sink, and speeded up the process by, as noted, cutting two holes in the deck so that the ship would go down immediately and not get in the way of other shipping.

The proceedings are difficult to follow. And, according to the young Belgian cook on the crew, he thought that the master had made the decision to abandon the ship before there was any decent reason to do so. The fact that the master had thrown out the kedge anchors was suspicious, as though he was ready for the sinking of the ship. The court believed that the cook had been bullied into saying these things by older members of the crew, who could not be trusted.

The crew had used threatening language to the master during arguments about the extra money they had demanded. In fact, it was said that one of the crew, during the hearing, made a groundless imputation about the master, which meant he had to be reproved for his conduct by the court.

The most mysterious figure in the story is the mate. Not one of the newspapers mentioned him by name. Even the crew lists are not clear. It's possible that he may have been Jenkin Jones of Aberaeron, who joined the crew of the *Rowland Evans* at Montevideo on 14 February 1882, towards the end of that difficult journey in South America, taking the place of Christopher Davenish. It seems a little unfair that he got censured for not having protested about the foolishness of the course the master was taking. Jenkin Jones was only 24 and inexperienced. Captain Evans was 54 and had sailed the world.

The final judgement was that no alteration of course was made for the purpose of approaching land, nor was there any vigorous exertion used to discover any leak. There was only one available pump, but that circumstance was entirely due to the master's negligence in proving that both pumps should be in working order when leaving Antwerp for Garston. The judge also took a strongly disapproving view of the log book being left behind on the sinking ship.

The punishment was to suspend Captain Evans' certificate for 12 calendar months from the date of the proceedings. The captain was unable to pay costs.

CHAPTER 21

Living with disgrace

NAIVELY, I EXPECTED that the following year he would once again have his master's certificate and he would able to work as a captain again. I was wrong. Most captains who had their reputations tarnished by a disciplinary hearing were rarely employed in that position again. John Evans tried to find gainful employment where he could, and his fellow master mariners did their best to support him. In 1886 he served as a lowly boatswain on the *Nathaniel* for £3.10 shillings a month. He claimed, when he filled in the crew list, that his previous ship had been the *Eleanor and Jane*, out of Aberystwyth. He does nor mention the *Rowland Evans*. The disgrace still rankled him.

The *Nathaniel* was not a grand ship. It was elderly, built in 1858 at Porthmadog. The shareholders were all Borth men who may have felt a little sympathy for John Evans. Captain Thomas Davies, who managed the ship, was, according to Terry Davies, a great lover of ships and women, and his seamanship was regarded with great respect by other mariners. When he arrived at port he would refuse the offer of a tug unless it was strictly necessary, and his crew were always dressed in their Sunday best. He would make his entrance into harbour with one hand on the wheel, and the other on the massive Bible he carried with him everywhere. Ironically, the *Nathaniel* was also eventually abandoned to sink 80 miles west of Fastnet in 1892.

John Evans' earlier reference to serving on the first *Eleanor and Jane* cannot be proved, but he did serve briefly on a voyage to Stettin on a second ship named *Eleanor and Jane*, in 1888. No doubt his earlier experience of visiting that difficult harbour would have served him well. His navigation skills had never been questioned, just his hasty decisions. The *Eleanor and Jane* was an impressive schooner, with the figurehead of a woman's chest and a framework of wood. However, its life was short. Built in 1884 in Padstow, Cornwall, it eventually foundered in 1892 off the Scilly Isles.

John Evans is named as the captain of a ship called *Savatele* in that famous photograph of Borth captains from about 1890, but there is no evidence. Maybe the photographer was confused (the name does sound like the name of a captain's house), although he got the names of the other ships correct. It appears that John Evans went to Newport, Monmouthshire, to find his last ship, the *Nelson Hewertson*, but again he was not the captain. The ship's captain's name was Llewellyn and the ship was originally registered in 1877.

*

John Evans died from the vengeance of the sea. He drowned on 12 December 1894, on a ship officially recorded as missing. At the bottom of the *Nelson Hewertson*'s register appears: 'Ship sailed from Nickerie on the 12th December 1894 and has not been heard of as per letter from William Brooks, the managing director, dated 8th April. Registry closed 8th April 1895.' More than likely, in that part of the world (Nickerie is in South America, present-day Suriname), the ship was the victim of a fierce hurricane.

There was no body to bring back to bury at his home, but a memorial stone was erected in his memory at Garn graveyard. A year later, when his wife Sarah died, she was buried under that same memorial. Much later, the eldest daughter Jane was buried there too. Sarah may well have died of a broken heart. To her, he was a 'worthy' captain and his daughters were always proud of him and kept alive his story.

No doubt they all attended the funeral swathed in black, as all those valiant women referred to as a Brân y Borth did. (This meant widows draped in black like crows; brân is Welsh for a crow). The village was full of women who had lost their menfolk and, sadly, also endured a high rate of infant mortality.

The expression Brân y Borth, however, got extended to anyone in Borth who showed independence of spirit. The captain's dear ladies had their own feisty independence, and kept alive the memory of their parents with great affection, if not always completely accurately. Had they kept knowledge about his disciplinary hearing from me because I was too young to understand? They must surely have been aware of how sad and humiliated he must have felt, no longer sailing ships as a captain. Not to mention the arduous work he was asked to do in the lower ranks as an older man.

Family memories are rarely kept alive absolutely accurately, but there is no doubting that the journeys of all those merchant ships were incredibly dangerous and required a special hardiness and courage in the men who sailed them.

My Thoughts

I felt somehow that I had to rescue his reputation.

To begin with, the *Rowland Evans* was in a state of decline on its last voyage. This is obvious when it's noted that a carpenter was on board during the first stage of the voyage, that the captain wanted to sell the ship when he arrived at Antwerp, that the anchors had needed to be replaced, and only one pump was working properly and a heavy cargo of silver sand only compounded matters.

Greater problems seem to have influenced the captain's decisions when he reached Cardigan Bay. Convinced that leaks were endangering the ship, he ordered the ship be abandoned, with his wife and crew taken into long boats. He genuinely felt danger for the loss of life.

I suspect two factors put him into a state of panic. He had vivid memories of the loss of his first ship, the schooner *Sarah*. He may also have been alarmed by his wife's fears. Unlike a lot of Borth women who travelled regularly on their husbands' ships, she only came to meet him infrequently and so was easily made nervous. It's not unlikely that she got hysterical in the circumstances. He may have felt that he should take her to the known safety of their home in Borth and to the family waiting there.

The captain's lawyer in court seemed to make a good point. Mr Lawrence said: 'his client may have committed an error of judgement in leaving the ship when he did, but it was ridiculous to suppose he had scuttled her, which was what the crew had tried to make out. That the boat had landed at the captain's house seemed merely a strange coincidence.'

It was indeed a picturesque detail that they had landed outside the captain's house, but maybe the wind had blown the rescue boat in that direction, for rescue boats boasted a little triangular sail at the front that would propel the boat forward. It was not such an unlikely journey to the centre of Cardigan Bay when the weather was reasonably calm. The captain may have thought it a very suitable place as it seemed a very direct route to him. Borth beach would have been so familiar, and Saxatile was in the very centre of the village. His knowledge would guarantee landing in the right place even in darkness. Above all, the captain's wife would have been frightened to take any other route.

It would, however, have been very annoying to the crew, most of whom came from Liverpool. How were they to get home? That long row to Borth must have been exhausting. If the captain only gave them their back pay, it would have seemed inadequate. However, somehow, they did catch the night mail to Liverpool. It's understandable that at the garden gate the crew became very ill-tempered. They were older men in their 40s and not easily bullied.

It was not as though Borth could offer them much. They would scarcely have felt comfortable in a village where most people only spoke Welsh. It may well have made them spiteful, although at least they were fed before they left and were given the passage home. The crew's surliness had not endeared them to the court hearing either, so their evidence was regarded as suspect. After all, one of the crew made a groundless imputation of the master, that meant he had to be reproved for his conduct. Again the crew would have been irritated at having to turn up in Swansea to give their evidence. Who paid their fares to get there?

How does the captain himself appear in all this? It's true he was never at ease with authority, and maybe gave himself airs. He might well have harboured a strong dislike of Englishmen. No doubt, being the third generation of a family of master mariners would have helped his self-confidence and made him impatient with men who did not have his experience of seafaring. It seems curious that, yet again, a missing log book had got the captain into hot water with shipping officials. The feeble excuse of mice and cockroaches having eaten it, as was claimed with the earlier missing log book, could scarcely be used again.

Officials were certainly obsessed with log books. They expected too much accuracy from sea captains whose literacy skills were erratic. It was more curious that he left behind on the ship his clothes and his instruments and charts (nautical instruments and charts were very expensive at that time). It sounds like he was panic-stricken, and taking the well-equipped medicine chest might have been a protection against accident. It was obviously very valuable. He may have genuinely been anxious about the loss of human life.

By the cynical standards of our time, there could have been

a stronger motive. He could have been hoping for the insurance to pay out. He was in financial difficulties as he was unable to pay the costs of the hearing and had already manoeuvred himself into paying two mortgages on the *Rowland Evans*. In the first year of the ship's life, he had that mortgage on 12 shares from a Mr Edwards, a London broker. In 1877, he had steadily been increasing his shares, so that he eventually owned 36 shares and had taken out another mortgage with a Morgan Owen of Aberystwyth, a ships' broker who became the official owner of the ship. In 1881 Morgan Owen sold six out of his 36 shares to his daughter. On the last crew list the name of the managing owner is left blank. In the 1882 parliamentary papers that gave the returns for the Board of Trade, a mysterious Mr Jones appears as the owner of the ship. Interestingly, it also mentioned that the ship was bound for Garston, the wind direction was NW4 and the place of casualty 25 miles SW half W of Bardsey Island, St George's Channel.

There is, of course, the problem of how accurate the newspapers were. The newspapers varied in the amount of detail given but all of the basic facts were, on the whole, consistent. Only the *Cambrian* gave an exact account of the state of the pumps and seems to have reported word for word the evidence of those taking part in the trial.

Like anyone who tries to solve the mystery of an abandoned ship, I had relied mainly on newspaper accounts of the time. Yet, there was something else that haunted me – I had also built a clear impression of the personalities of Captain John Evans and his wife from what I had heard from my family. I did feel that I had a special insight into what happened that day off Bardsey Island...

Praise Song to Cardigan Bay and its Master Mariners

We know your songs,
We have heard your bells
And seen in the wooden stumps
The magic of those ancient times.

We know your legends
We have heard of Cantref Gwaelod
And seen on the bobbing waves
The crane-skin bag that brought Taliesin home.

We know of the women waiting
For the men's herring boats
And seen their children's starved faces
And wretched hungry bodies

We know the ships that were built
On the shores of Dyfi
And the men with whom we sailed
To the many corners of the world.

We know the coming of the laughing youngsters
With buckets and spades in hand
Who run on our golden sand
And laugh at the water between their toes.

And as the sun sets
Borth is alive with more dreams
Our captains' ghosts come. Trailing behind them
Are their women in their crow-like black.

Oh! Those magic foaming waves
Have fed my imagination
And have filled my head with visions
I now must tell to you.

Appendix

Sources

Elizabeth Allen, *Glenlee: Life at Sea under Sail*

Terry Davies, *Borth: A seabourne village* (2004)

Terry Davies, *Borth: A maritime history* (2009)

Terry Davies, *borthmaritimehistory.com*

Basil Greenhill and Denis Stonham, *Seafaring under Sail* (1982)

Chris Holden, online research into the loss of the *Rowland Evans*

David Jenkins, 'Shipping and Ship Building' in *Cardiganshire County History*, Volume III (1998)

David Jenkins, 'Shipbuilding and ship owning in Montgomeryshire – the Evans family of Morben Isaf'

Hubert Lampo, *Antwerpen Gefotografeerd* (1976)

Beryl Lewis, 'The Buildings of Morfa Borth' (Ceredigion Archives)

David Marcombe, *The Victorian Sailor* (1985)

D.W. Morgan, *Brief Glory: The Story of a Quest* (1948)

Thomas Love Peacock, *The Misfortunes of Elphin* (1829)

Peter Stevenson, *Ceredigion Folk Tales* (2014)

Peter Stevenson, *Welsh Folk Tales* (2017)

George Van Cauwenbergh, *Antwerp: Portrait of a Port* (1983)

Census returns, 1851–1901

Welsh Mariners Index, 1845–1930

Dates of nineteenth-century Borth

1789: Borth put on the map by cartographer Jon Cary, under the name of Porth

1800: Building of Calvinist Methodist chapel, Soar

1801: Libanus Sunday school opens

1804: Soar moves into the main village

1806: Shiloh Wesleyan Methodist chapel built; old chapel becomes the British School (later Upper Borth Primary School)

1828: Lewis Edwards buys the sloop *France*, the beginning of local men acquiring ships

1842: *Mary and Ellen* and *Mary Rees* are the first ships to be built on the newly diverted Leri river

First very small schooner (30 tons) built on Borth's foreshore

1845: Apportionment of rent in lieu of taxes act so each property throughout Britain to be mapped and scheduled

1854: Sinking of the large fishing boat *Ruth* under the cliffs at Borth

1857: Storms meant the loss of small fishing boats, leaving seven widows and 20 children behind

1863: Machynlleth to Borth section of the railway line built

1864: Borth to Aberystwyth line built

1865: St Mathew's Church of Wales church built

1876: Great storms

The Evans Family tree

John Evans 1763–1808 m. Sarah

|

John Evans 1792–1853 m. Mary Benjamin

|

John Evans 1828–94 m. Sarah Jones – Jane – Sarah Elizabeth
m. Thomas Lloyd

|

William John
Jane
Sarah Mary
Margaretta Elizabeth
Thomas

So how do I fit in.? Sarah became the second wife of W.T. Lewis. My mother and her brother Alfie were the children of W.T. Lewis and his first wife Annie Mary Farquar Evans, a beauty with ravishing red hair whom he married in 1901 and who died in 1913 He obviously married the down-to-earth Sarah Mary Evans to take care of his motherless children. My mother married my father during the Second World War. They had a simple wartime wedding and I was an only child born three years later, in 1943.

The contents of Captain Evans' medicine chest

THE MEDICINE	What it was	What it cured
Cold Drawn Castor oil	Vegetable oil from castor bean	Constipation
Black Draught	A mixture including senna, spirit of lavender, Epsom salts and harts thorn to preserve it	Constipation
Quinine	Made from the bark of the cinchona in Peru	Reducing fever, curing malaria
Bicarbonate of soda	A chemical compound added to water	Acid ingestion and heart burn and constipation
Rhubarb Powder	Made from the plant	Constipation
Tincture of Rhubarb	Alcohol added	Constipation
Flowers of Sulphur	More commonly known as brimstone and was an anti-fungus and an antiseptic. Taken with treacle 'to sort you out'	Itching from lice or help with healing wounds
Tartaric Acid	Found in grapes, bananas and wine	Relaxing muscles
Poison Laudanum	Alcoholic herbal preparation containing opium and codeine	Suppresses cough
Nitrates of Potash	Commonly known as saltpetre and found in gunpowder	
Diarrhoea Powder		Obvious
Tincture of Henbane	Herb	Sedative effect often used to relieve toothache
Dovers powder	Includes powdered opium and morphine	Colds and fever
Poison Lunar Caustic	Silver nitrate to be made into sticks as a cauterizing agent	Disinfects wounds
Oil of Aniseed	Made from an umbelliferous plant	Used as a cordial
Opium pills	Made from poppies	Pain relief

Captain Evans and his ships

The *Sarah*
Registered 1858
Tonnage 106
1858–63: Crew lists at Greenwich Library
1864: Crew list at National Library of Wales
Vessel lost 9 April 1864, Bay of Biscay
Ship lost, crew saved

The *Rowland Evans*
Tonnage 208
Ship's register at Ceredigion Archives
1866–74: Crew lists at National Library of Wales
1875: Crew list at Greenwich Library
1876–82: Crew lists at National Library of Wales

Eleanor and Jane
Tonnage 110
1888: Crew list at National Library of Wales

Nelson Hewertson
1894: Ship's register

Ships built by the Evans family of Morben Isaf at Derwenlas and Aberdyfi

1852: 76-ton gross schooner *Sarah and Mary*, Derwenlas

1853: 43-ton gross smack *Seven Brothers*, Derwenlas

1855: 97-ton gross schooner *Miss Evans*, Derwenlas

1856: Rowland Evans dies

1860: 94-ton gross schooner *Deborah*, Derwenlas

1860: 90-ton gross schooner *Idris*, Aberdyfi

1861: 38-ton gross smack *Morben*, Aberdyfi

1864 112-ton gross schooner *Acorn*, Aberdyfi

1865–7: 208-ton gross brig *Rowland Evans*, Derwenlas

1867: 67-ton gross barque *Mary Evans*, Derwenlas

1868: John Evans dies

Note:

For all ships, the shipbuilder was John Jones, Jac y Traeth, except for *Idris* which was built by Evan Owen.

The Cambrian newspaper articles

THE CAMBRIAN, 6 October 1882

ABANDONMENT OF THE BRIG *ROWLAND EVANS*
BOARD OF TRADE INQUIRY AT SWANSEA YESTERDAY

At the Guildhall, at noon yesterday, Mr J. C. Fowler sat as judge, with Captains Thos. Beasley and Robert Harland as nautical assessors, to inquire by order of the Board of Trade, into the case of the abandonment and total loss of the brig *Rowland Evans*. Mr. E. Strick (Stricks and Bellingham) appeared on behalf of the Board of Trade, to conduct the proceedings, and Mr. W. Lawrence (Smith and Lawrence), represented the owners and John Evans, the master. In his opening statement, Mr. E. Strick said the *Rowland Evans* was a brig, built at Derwen-lass, in Montgomeryshire, in 1865. At that time, John Evans superintended the building, and was the principal owner. She was classed Al at Lloyd's for 12 years. Her registered tonnage was 209 tons, her official number was 53,031; length, 101 feet; breadth, 25 feet, and depth 13 feet. According to the last register, which was in November 1881, it appeared that Mr. Evans owned 36 / 64ths, and that they were mortgaged for £600. The remaining shares were spread over eight different persons as owners. The brig on her last voyage was bound from Antwerp to Garston, in Lancashire, with a cargo of silver sand. It appeared that on the outer voyage, she had put into Falmouth, where she was inspected by Lloyd's surveyor, and caulked from the copper up to the ways. She then went in tow of a tug to Antwerp, with a cargo of hides. When she had been laden with silver sand, she came down to Flushing Roads where she lay at anchor until her chain parted. The master then ran her up the river to Ternoose, where she lost another anchor. Eventually she was provided with two new ones. It was a question whether she had not previously made a good deal of water. On the 5th September she again commenced her voyage, and then it appeared she made a great deal of water. On the 6th and the following days, the pumps got out of order. When she got off the Welsh coast, the master and crew abandoned her twice, and went back to her twice, after an absence of an hour or so. Finally, they abandoned her altogether about 18 miles south-west of Bardsey Island, and the captain and crew landed at Borth, on the Cardiganshire coast, which curiously enough was his home. Now it was a curious coincidence that this ship should have brought them safely to the captain's home. The Stipendiary Magistrate said it reminded him of the lady who went out bathing at Ventnor, met her husband coming home from the West Indies. (Laughter.) Mr. Strick added that the brig had not been seen to go down, but before leaving her the crew had made holes in her deck so as to sink her, they said, out of the way of the navigation. The master estimated the vessel to be worth £2,000, and the cargo at £80; and the ship was insured for £1,800. A little evidence in support of this statement was taken, and the court adjourned at half-past one o'clock until today (Friday).

THE CAMBRIAN, 13 October 1882

THE ABANDONMENT OF THE BRIG *ROWLAND EVANS*. UN-SEAMANLIKE CONDUCT OF THE CAPTAIN.

The Board of Trade inquiry into the circumstances connected with the abandonment of the brig *Rowland Evans* concluded on Monday, when the Stipendiary Magistrate (J. Coke Fowler, Esq.) delivered the following judgment of the Court. The nautical assessors were Captains Beasley and Hartland. Mr. Edward Strick, solicitor, appeared for the Board of Trade, and Mr. Lawrence (Smith and Lawrence) for the captain and mate. The brig was laden with a cargo of silver sand, was on a voyage from Antwerp to Garston, in Lancashire, and was abandoned on the 12th of September on the Welsh coast.

The Board of Trade submitted the following questions to the Court, the replies to which, and the opinion of the Stipendiary and the assessors, we now append:

1. Whether, when the vessel left Antwerp she was in good and seaworthy condition? – We propose to connect this question with No. 5, and answer them together.

2. Whether she was properly supplied with anchors and chains, and whether they were in good condition? – Yes.

3. Whether the pumps were in good and proper working order and properly equipped? – Decidedly not. The evidence shows that there was only one break for the two pumps, and, in fact, the two were never worked simultaneously.

4. Whether, when the vessel left Flushing Roads on the 6th September, she was in good and seaworthy condition? – We also connect this question with No. 1 and No. 5.

5. Whether, having regard to the statement of the mate, that the vessel made 6, or 7 inches of water per hour while being towed from Falmouth to Antwerp, the master was justified in neglecting to have repairs effected before again proceeding to sea, especially with such a heavy and dead-weight cargo as silver sand? – The master was not justified in proceeding to sea without having her overhauled and repaired.

6. What was the cause of the water suddenly increasing on the night of the 11th September? – There is no evidence to show the cause.

7. What was the cause of the sudden increase of water in the well from 2 feet at 9.30 p.m., to 6 feet at 12.30 a.m. on the following morning? – We are not satisfied that the water did rise to the height of 6 feet.

8. Whether every possible effort was made to ascertain the cause of and to stop the leak?

   – No energetic effort seems to have been made.

9. Whether every possible effort was made to keep the water under?

   – We think that further exertions ought to have been made to keep the water under.

10. Whether, when it was discovered that the water could not be kept under, the course of the vessel should not have been altered with a view to her reaching a port in Cardigan Bay or to beach her in Borth Sands?

    – Certainly that course ought to have been adopted.

11. With what object were the kedge anchors put out?

    – We are utterly at a loss to know. The captain could offer no satisfactory explanation of this order.

12. What were the circumstances in which the master ordered the mate and seamen to cut up the decks and knock off the scupper pipes, and whether he was justified in so doing?

    – There were no circumstances which warranted the master in ordering the decks to be cut and knocking off the scupper pipes, and he certainly was not justified in doing so.

13. Whether every possible effort was made to save the vessel?

    – Decidedly not; no effort whatever seems to have been made.

14. Whether the vessel was navigated with proper and seamanlike care?

    – Up to about 10 p.m. of the 11th of September we find she was properly navigated.

15. Whether she was prematurely abandoned?

16. And finally, whether the master and mate, or either, and which of them is or are in default, and whether blame attaches to any other person?

    – She was prematurely abandoned.

The Court finds that the master is in default, and also that the mate is answerable for not making some protest at the time against unwarrantable acts. In the opinion of the Board of Trade, the certificates of the master and mate should be dealt with.

The Stipendiary added: I think it desirable to add a few explanatory comments upon the facts of this case. It is the clearest example of premature abandonment that has ever come under my notice.

Whoever has heard and read, as I have, numerous narratives of other abandonments; of masters clinging to their vessels in mid-ocean when spars, masts and sails have been carried away, or rudders injured, or pumps going night and day; cargo jettisoned and baling resorted to, in tempestuous weather and mountainous seas, must be astonished to hear the history of the *Rowland Evans*. For she was abandoned in fine weather, with a calm sea and a favourable breeze, every spar and sail intact, two excellent boats, the pumps still throwing some water, an obedient crew, and within 28 or 30 miles of the visible Cardiganshire coast, offering two or three places which the brig might have approached with safety. Yet no alteration of the course was made for the purpose of approaching the land, nor can I learn that any vigorous exertion was used either to discover any leak, to bale, or to jettison. Undoubtedly, there was only one available pump, but that circumstance was entirely due to the master's negligence in not providing that both pumps (which may well be called the life of the ship) should be in working order when one left Antwerp for Garston. It does not even appear that any serious consultation as to the abandonment ever took place between Captain Evans and his mate. Neither was the pumping continued with any continuous energy after midnight. We were told by the master that he decided to leave her because she was sinking. This statement is certainly incorrect.

He put his wife and the crew into the long boat, and from

that boat he boarded the brig again and again, and finally cut through her deck and covering boards to hasten her disappearance. He then steered the boat for the Cardiganshire coast, but so far was the brig from sinking that she remained afloat as long as she could be seen by the departing crew, and although she was boarded again and again, it is an extraordinary fact that the ship's log was left in the ship. Thus, it appears upon the undisputed facts that the brig was clearly abandoned while a reasonable chance, nay a moral certainty, remained of taking her to some part of the Welsh shore, and, considering the state of the wind and tide, it is even probable that if she had not been wilfully injured, she might herself have drifted to the coast before the following night. If we accept the evidence of the crew, and especially that of a young Belgian cook, the case assumes a far worse aspect. For if he spoke the truth, it follows that the master was contemplating and preparing for the abandonment before any decent pretext existed.

The fact that he threw out kedge anchors and can only explain it by saying that he did so under excitement; that he must (as I think) have intentionally left the log in the ship; that he never set a course to near the shore, and that he cut open her deck, all tend to confirm that supposition. But, on the other hand we are told that some of the crew used threatening language when the master refused some small payment after landing them at Borth. One of them made a groundless imputation on the master, for which I rebuked him severely. On the whole, I do not feel able to rely with confidence on their evidence, and it is not very improbable that the boy was influenced as to his evidence by them. We therefore give the master the benefit of the doubt that arises as to the accuracy of every statement made by the crew, and simply say that we are satisfied that he grievously failed in the discharge of the primary duty of a master, namely to cling to his vessel to the last, and never abandon her except under the pressure of immediate danger to life. Under these circumstances, attaching as they do much blame to Captain Evans, the Court finds him in default, and suspends his certificate for 12 calendar months from this date. With regard to the mate, the court thinks him liable to censure for not protesting at the time against the course taken, and he is censured accordingly.

The value of the vessel was estimated at £2,000 the cargo £80. The ship was insured for £1,800; the captain was the principal owner, but his shares were mortgaged for £800.

Mr. Strick applied for costs as against the captain, but Mr. Lawrence said he would be unable to pay.

The Court made no order as to costs.

Also from Y Lolfa:

GWYN JENKINS

A WELSH COUNTY AT WAR

ESSAYS ON CEREDIGION AT THE TIME OF THE FIRST WORLD WAR

y Lolfa

£9.99

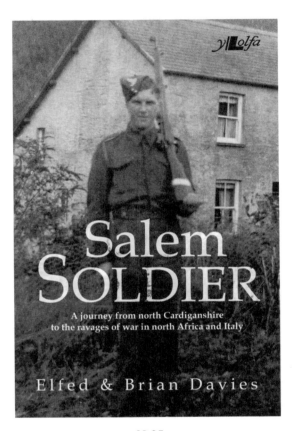

Salem SOLDIER

A journey from north Cardiganshire
to the ravages of war in north Africa and Italy

Elfed & Brian Davies

£9.95

LAND OF LEAD

THE STORY OF FOUR GENERATIONS OF A NORTH CEREDIGION FAMILY

BRIAN DAVIES

y Lolfa

£9.99

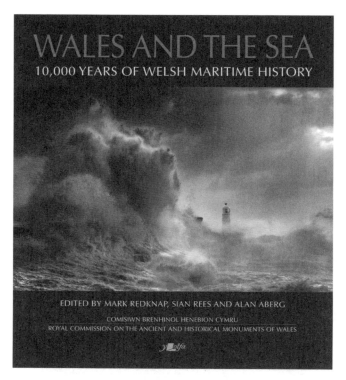

WALES AND THE SEA
10,000 YEARS OF WELSH MARITIME HISTORY

EDITED BY MARK REDKNAP, SIAN REES AND ALAN ABERG

COMISIWN BRENHINOL HENEBION CYMRU
ROYAL COMMISSION ON THE ANCIENT AND HISTORICAL MONUMENTS OF WALES

y Lolfa

£24.99

Ask for a print quote!
www.ylolfa.com